FAITH R

Faith and

Stephen Bullivant

CANTERBURY

PRESS

Norwich

© Stephen Bullivant 2013

First published in 2013 by the Canterbury Press Norwich
Editorial office
3rd Floor, Invicta House
108–114 Golden Lane
London EC1Y 0TG

Canterbury Press is an imprint of Hymns Ancient & Modern Ltd
(a registered charity)
13A Hellesdon Park Road, Norwich
Norfolk, NR6 5DR, UK

www.canterburypress.co.uk

British Library Cataloguing in Publication data

A catalogue record for this book is available
from the British Library

978 1 84825 280 6

Typeset by The Manila Typesetting Company
Printed and bound in Great Britain by
CPI Group (UK) Ltd, Croydon CR0 4YY

Contents

Introduction by the FAITH GOING DEEPER series editor

Academic theology is in good heart in these early years of the twenty-first century: much Christian thinking is confident and vigorous; there is more enthusiasm for theology among the clergy than for some decades. All the same, the work that theologians produce is not always accessible to those who should be its principal beneficiaries: the people of the Church.

With this series, *Faith Going Deeper*, the aim is to provide a bridge for Christians of all traditions to some of what is most valuable and significant in contemporary theological thinking and writing. In doing so, the series will also introduce some younger theologians to a wider, popular audience. The books deal with central themes of Christian thought and life, starting with grace, virtue, faith and the sacraments. Their authors aim to be clear without being simplistic, and to avoid technical terms while providing a framework for understanding the subject in hand. They are assured in the truth of the Christian faith, and on that basis unafraid to face the challenges of our times.

The writers of these books, and I as the editor of the series, agree with the point Dorothy L. Sayers never tired of making, that nothing rejuvenates the mission of the Church like contact with good Christian theology. Our faith is far from dull; as Sayers put it, 'it is the neglect of dogma that makes for dullness'. With these books we hope to present again what she called 'the Divine Drama', so that it might once again 'startle the world'. That will only happen if it first of all startles the Church once again.

Andrew Davison
Cambridge
Eastertide 2012

To Mary Jo and Tom Gornick,
and Claire and Ron Woodruff,
with thanks

Acknowledgements

The idea for this book arose out of a lecture given at St Stephen's House, University of Oxford, as part of a summer school held in June 2009. I am grateful to Fr Andrew Davison both for that initial invitation, and for the subsequent suggestion to write this book. Sincere thanks are also due to Christine Smith at Canterbury Press, without whose early encouragement this volume would never have been. Throughout the whole process – from offering helpful comments on draft proposals, to giving clement replies to apologies for the lateness of the final manuscript – both Christine and Andrew have been a joy to work with. For making the American edition happen, I wish to express my gratitude to Donna Crilly and Fr Mark-David Janus at Paulist Press.

Over the past year or so, colleagues at St Mary's University College – particularly Ashley Beck, Leonora Butau, David Fincham, Robin Gibbons, Cathy Hobday, John Lydon, Paul Rowan, Trevor Stammers, Anthony Towey, Káren Towey and Peter Tyler – have created, at times seemingly against all the odds, a congenial atmosphere for thinking and writing. Others at St Mary's have also played crucial roles on this score, not least the students taking my 'Atheism and Nonreligion' module over the past three years, and the community at Benedict XVI House: Leonora and Rufaro Butau,

Berna Durcan, Alice Costar, Jasmine Garcia, Jacinta Rhodes, Agnes Swamba and Hannah Young. Thanks to you all.

Whatever its present faults – for which I take sole responsibility – *Faith and Unbelief* would be very much the worse were it not for the generous and insightful comments of Jo Bullivant, Fr Andrew Davison, Deacon Tom Gornick and Fr Greg Murphy OP on various rough-hewn drafts. There is scarcely a page that has not benefitted, in many cases very greatly, from their winnowing forks. I have also been blessed with the opportunity to try out my developing ideas on the readers of *America*, an honour for which I am chiefly grateful to Fr Matt Malone SJ and Kerry Weber.

In addition, earlier versions of some of my thoughts and examples have appeared as: 'Atheism, Apologetics and Ecclesiology: *Gaudium et Spes* and Contemporary Unbelief', in Andrew Davison (ed.), 2011, *Imaginative Apologetics: Theology, Philosophy and the Catholic Tradition*, London: SCM Press, pp. 81–97; and 'Christian Spirituality and Atheism', in Richard Woods and Peter Tyler (eds), 2012, *The Bloomsbury Guide to Christian Spirituality*, London: Bloomsbury, pp. 375–86.

Lastly, the key themes of Chapter 6 were first aired for a talk entitled 'Putting the New Evangelization into Practice (By Putting Practice into the New Evangelization)', at the Archdiocese of Portland's annual catechetical conference in October 2012. In gratitude for that invitation, a wonderful week exploring Oregon, and their lasting friendship, this book is dedicated to Mary Jo and Tom Gornick, and Claire and Ron Woodruff.

Stephen Bullivant
Nottingham, UK
Feast of Sts Perpetua and Felicity, 2013

Introduction

The Greek word *atheos*, the root of the English 'atheist', appears only once in the whole New Testament. St Paul chides the Christians at Ephesus, reminding these former pagans of when they were 'without Christ, being aliens from the commonwealth of Israel, and strangers to the covenants of promise, having no hope and *atheoi* in the world' (Eph. 2.12). Yet quite what Paul means by the term, used here in the plural, is by no means clear. Most Bible translations render it as 'without God', which is the literal definition: a combination of *a-*, signifying a 'lack' or 'absence' (as in amoral or asexual), and *-theos* as the normal Greek word for a god or God.

But 'without God(s)' in what sense exactly? Paul might mean that the Ephesian converts were *without a belief in the existence of* the Christian God, or of the pagan gods, or of both God and the gods. Or he might mean 'without God(s)' in the sense of his/their having abandoned the future Ephesian converts to their own devices (the English word 'godforsaken' originally carried something of this meaning). Or he might mean it in an extended sense, as a negative, moral judgement on their previous lifestyles ('godless' or 'ungodly'). All these meanings, referring to either the Judeo-Christian God, or the Greco-Roman gods, were possible in at least some forms of ancient Greek. Which of them, if any, Paul had in mind, he doesn't however make plain.

One thing we can be fairly sure of, however, is that Paul's erstwhile *atheoi* were not 'atheists' in anything like the modern meaning(s) of the term. While the word can and does carry a range of definitions, associations and connotations, it is normally used today in two main ways. The first refers to people who are without a belief in the existence of a God or gods; this is sometimes called 'negative' or 'weak' atheism. The second, more narrowly, refers only to those who believe – with varying degrees of strength and conviction – that there is no God or gods; this is sometimes called 'positive' or 'strong' atheism. Generally speaking, this book favours the first, broader definition – one *includes* agnostics and people who have never given the issue a moment's thought, as well as all of the positive atheists too. Much that is said in these pages will also apply to the far larger group of people who also have or feel no formal affiliation to a religion. Most religious 'nones', as they are sometimes called, are not actual atheists or nonbelievers; perhaps two-thirds of them typically affirm some kind of belief in a God or gods. But since many of them share the same criticisms and suspicions of Christianity that many atheists have, a good deal of this book will apply to them also, even though they will not be our direct focus here.

It is important to realize, from the outset, that not all atheists are 'the same'. Just as there is a great deal of diversity both between and within different groups of theists, so too is there between different groups of atheists, whether 'negative' or 'positive'. Nevertheless, they all share one significant common feature: all are *without a belief in the existence of a God or gods*.

Paul's 'atheists'

Almost certainly, such was not the case with Paul's Ephesian Christians-to-be. As ordinary inhabitants of the Greco-Roman world, and moreover living in a city famous for its cult of the goddess Artemis (see Acts 19), it is highly unlikely that they would have lacked belief in the existence and importance of gods. They were polytheists, and not – or not in the usual way the word is understood now – atheists at all. It is also worth noting that Paul is not *really* talking about the Ephesians' former religious beliefs and practices. His emphasis is instead on what they have gained from their new religion: the abundance of gifts and privileges that the Lord has heaped upon them, unworthy though they may be, and which (Paul fears) they are in danger of forgetting in the midst of their petty squabbles and backsliding into old ways. As such, he paints – with rather broad brushstrokes – a picture of how their former pagan lives compare to their new life in Christ: hopeless and godless.

There is a certain rhetorical artifice to Paul's exhortation, however. For he is also, in different moods and to different ends, quite capable of finding positives in pagan living. When speaking to the Athenians at the Areopagus, the author of Acts tells us, he is quite comfortable identifying the pagan idol 'to an unknown God' as pointing, however indirectly, to the one true God: 'What therefore you worship as unknown, this I proclaim to you' (17.23). Likewise, in his letter to the Romans, he acknowledges that there are Gentiles who have 'what the law requires . . . written on their hearts, to which their own conscience also bears witness' (2.15). These pagans and Gentiles at least, as much *atheoi* as the Ephesians used to be, seem not to be such unqualifiedly hopeless, godless cases after all.

Paul's comment in Ephesians is not directly translatable to the Christian understanding of contemporary atheism or unbelief (terms I use interchangeably, as both signifying an absence of belief in the existence of a God or gods). Nevertheless, his use of *atheos* is instructive in other respects. First, it should caution us against the ambiguity of key terms. Just as it is not immediately obvious what Paul intends by *atheos*, we must also be aware that 'atheist' can be used in different ways. For most of western history it has been used almost exclusively as an insult – prior to the nineteenth century (and in many places, long after), it is rare to find people describing themselves as such. Conversely, it is surprisingly common to find people who certainly were not atheists in the modern sense being so labelled, among them Socrates, the early Christian martyrs and Martin Luther.

Second, from the perspective of the Christian faith – a perspective to which I hope to do justice in this book – Paul is undoubtedly right that being *atheos*, at least in the sense of being 'without *God*', is far from optimal. As we have seen, that didn't prevent Paul recognizing the conspicuous positives among the cultured Athenians or those righteous Gentiles who are 'a law to themselves' (Rom. 2.14). In the same way, this does not prevent Christians from recognizing that atheism can be, and very often is, compatible with living a rational, meaningful and morally virtuous life. There may even be atheist saints. But even so, *if Christianity is true*, then atheists – along with all other non-Christians – must surely, at the very minimum, be missing out on something of supreme significance. Christianity proclaims not only that there *is* a God, but that this God became a human being, lived among us for three decades, was executed as a political criminal and rose again from the dead. If these claims are true, then they must surely be among the profoundest and most far-reaching facts that human beings are capable of discovering. As such, all people who have yet to 'come to the knowledge of the truth' (1 Tim. 2.4), in many cases undoubtedly through no fault of their own, are the worse for it. Quite why this is so, and what implications it has for Christian thought and practice, is explored later in this book.

But let us not get ahead of ourselves. The reason why Paul, in common with the other biblical writers, has little to say *directly* to the theology of contemporary atheism is very obvious. Unbelief, in anything like the modern sense of the word, was a very rare phenomenon indeed in the ancient world. While not altogether unknown – we know of a handful of philosophers who fit more or less easily into this bracket – atheism was not a live 'option' for the vast majority of people.[1] Broadly speaking, the same could be said for the best part of the next two thousand years, at least in the west. Situations such as we find today in much of Europe, North America (increasingly) and elsewhere, where large proportions of the population have no belief in a God or gods, would have been scarcely conceivable to such perceptive and imaginative figures from the Christian tradition as Justin Martyr, Augustine, Pseudo-Dionysius the Areopagite, Meister Eckhart and Thomas Aquinas. (Although that need not stop us accepting and developing some of their ideas for our very different intellectual and social milieu.) While there is much in the modern world

---

1 For example, in the opening paragraphs of Romans, Paul seems to imply that, given the overwhelming evidence provided by Creation itself, theoretical atheism is not a genuine possibility: 'For what can be known about God is plain to them, because God has shown it to them. Ever since the creation of the world his eternal power and divine nature, invisible though they are, have been understood and seen through the things he has made. So they are without excuse' (1.19–20).

that would surprise and amaze them, it is perhaps this fact, above all, that they would find most astonishing.

A world of atheism

Atheism today is a large, pervasive, growing and – by now – perfectly 'ordinary' feature of a great many societies. Though this is not the place to delve too deeply into statistics, according to findings from the 2008 International Social Survey Programme (ISSP), 14% of Britons claimed: 'I don't believe in God', while a further 16% affirmed: 'I don't believe in God and I don't believe there is a way to find out'. Both groups, of course, count as 'atheists' in our definition, even if a great many of these people wouldn't choose to use that label of themselves. Europe as a whole, as it happens, shows a great deal of variation. Cyprus had the lowest incidence, with a combined total of 5% in the two atheistic categories, closely followed by Portugal (8%), and Poland and Ireland (both 9%). At the opposite end of the spectrum were the Czech Republic (52%), Sweden (39%), France (37%) and Germany (34%). Britain's combined total of 30% brought it in as eighth overall. By contrast, only 8% of Americans were 'without a belief in the existence of a God or gods' in 2008. It is worth noting, however, that the US population that year was around 305 million: even so comparatively low a proportion of unbelievers still adds up to over 25 million Americans.[2]

---

2 A more recent, widely reported Pew Forum study in 2012 found that 5.7% of American adults would self-describe as either an atheist or an agnostic. As noted above, and for interesting reasons that need not detain us, large numbers of people who are de facto atheists or agnostics shy away from describing themselves with those labels. Even this lower

The sheer existence of unbelief on this scale poses Christianity and its followers with a large number of important and uncomfortable questions. Consider the fact that all of the above countries are (or *were* in the not too distant past) predominantly Christian nations. These are not places where Christ has never been proclaimed, or where the Church has never been able to gain a decent foothold. In the case of Europe, these countries were at the heart of 'Christendom' for the best part of the last two thousand years. And yet today, large and increasing sectors of their populations (often among the young) are not only not Christians any more, but in many cases are no longer even theists. There are many and varied reasons and explanations for this – historical, sociological, political, philosophical – several of which we will explore in Chapters 2 and 3. Yet for the time being it is worth reflecting on a single observation: that, generally speaking, largescale societal unbelief is a hallmark of Christian, or historically Christian, countries. There are several notable exceptions to this, of course. For example: there were strong atheistic traditions in ancient India; several strands of Buddhism are arguably atheistic in at least the negative sense of the world; and China, Vietnam and North Korea all have large unbelieving populations (influenced by ideologies that arose and gained prominence in Christian regions). But the basic point holds nevertheless. This recognition alone ought to be enough for us to take atheism seriously as a topic for theological enquiry.

---

figure, however, combined with a 2012 adult population estimate of around 228 million, yields almost 13 million people. For further details, please see: www.pewforum.org/unaffiliated/nones-on-the-rise.aspx.

Scope, perspective and outline

Contemporary western unbelief – in all its many forms,
some less visible than others – presents Christians with
a large number of significant and significantly interesting
questions. These range from the philosophical and apologetic ('can an honest and rational person still believe in
God?'), to the ecclesiological ('to what extent has Christian
thought and/or practice motivated or enabled the rising
tide of unbelief?'), to the soteriological ('can my unbelieving daughter, father, wife or friend be saved?'), to the
missiological ('how can Christians, individually and collectively, present the good news in a world of unbelief?'), to
the dialogical ('what can Christians learn from atheists and
vice versa?'), and beyond.

The purpose of this short book is to serve as an introduction to these issues, plus several more besides. It is a book
about faith and unbelief, by a (Roman Catholic) Christian,
and is *primarily* written with other Christians (of all kinds)
in mind. Its main intention is to communicate some serious theological reflection on contemporary unbelief to
'the people of the Church'. For this and stylistic reasons,
I often speak in the first person plural ('we' or 'our') when
referring to 'Christians in general', rather than in the more
'distant' third person ('they' or 'their') – as, for example, in
the title of Chapter 3: 'Is it not our own fault?' I hope that
any readers who are not themselves Christians do not find
this irritating or needlessly excluding.

There has been no shortage of books written by Christian
philosophers or theologians on atheism and related issues
in recent years. Indeed, it sometimes seems as though
theologians especially have written about little else in the
past half-decade or so. And while some of these have been

rather good, they have tended to deal almost exclusively with something called the 'New Atheism'. The precise nature and scope of this phenomenon is hard to define, but bestselling books by Sam Harris (*The End of Faith*, *Letter to a Christian Nation*), Richard Dawkins (*The God Delusion*), Christopher Hitchens (*God is Not Great*) and Daniel Dennett (*Breaking the Spell*) are some of its most characteristic and famous expressions. It is these authors who philosophers and theologians have tended to focus on – and understandably so. Their responses have, moreover, been primarily apologetic (if not outrightly polemical) in nature.

Apologetics is a noble and necessary calling – 'Always be ready to make your defence to anyone who demands from you an account of the hope that is in you; yet do it with gentleness and reverence' (1 Peter 3.15–16) – and Dawkins, Dennett, Harris and Hitchens are worthy intellectual foils, and socially, culturally and politically significant. And yet the New Atheism is by no means co-extensive with contemporary western atheism; it is but one relatively vocal manifestation of a far broader and more subtle phenomenon. (Only fairly small percentages of the unbelievers we identified in the ISSP statistics would identify with the content and tone of *The God Delusion*, for example. And there is at least some sociological evidence to suggest that agnostic atheists, in particular, tend to be especially critical of the book.) And so while apologetics is undoubtedly important, it does not exhaust the challenges that unbelief poses for the Christian. The scope of the numerous Christian theological engagements with world religions goes far beyond establishing how they are *wrong*. So too, therefore, must Christian theological engagements with contemporary atheism. Hence although the New Atheist authors will, on occasion, be mentioned or quoted, this present volume will concentrate on *other* topics at the interface, or fault line, between the Christian faith and our modern-day 'culture of unbelief'.

This book is divided into six chapters. Chapter 1 starts to open up the, perhaps surprising, possibilities of a constructive, theological engagement with atheistic thought. Titled 'The "atheism" of Christianity', the central point is the bold contention that the Christian God is not a god – an assertion that might just be radical *enough* to be fully orthodox. This opens a number of intriguing theological possibilities. These must be treated with due caution and sophistication, since naive misunderstandings are possible on either side. Nevertheless, the idea is an important one, and throws into sharp focus both the affinities and genuine differences between Christianity and unbelief.

Chapter 2 takes up a central contention of this book: that atheism, while false, is a legitimate and reasonable belief held by many open-minded, virtuous and intelligent people. Unless this is recognized, Christians cannot hope to engage with modern unbelief in any serious or successful way. To aid this, this chapter looks at three common intellectual causes of atheism (and religious doubt in general): the scandalous nature of the gospel, suffering and evil, and the apparent sufficiency of scientific explanations. The primary motive is understanding rather than refutation: 'why do so many people find the existence of God so implausible?' That said, attempt is made to place these objections within a properly Christian theological context. Building on these philosophical reasons for atheism, Chapter 3 explores the ways in which Christians themselves, individually and collectively, may be responsible for the rise, spread and plausibility of unbelief. The issues broached are both intellectual (inadequacies of catechesis, apologetics and evangelization) and practical (religious hypocrisy, complicity in unjust social/political structures and failing 'to live as though the Truth were true').

Undoubtedly the weightiest question that atheism throws up for Christian theology – not least for those with unbelieving friends and relatives (i.e. everyone?) – is the question of salvation. The path walked in Chapter 4 is between presumption on the one hand and pessimism on the other. Without becoming too mired in technical issues, I draw upon Scripture and tradition to justify the view that some unbelievers can and will fulfil the traditional, orthodox criteria for salvation of faith, baptism, and the mediation of the Church (assuming they want to be saved: itself an interesting question). The wider *hope* that ultimately all human beings will be saved is also discussed, with reference to the ideas of the Catholic theologian Hans Urs von Balthasar (*Dare We Hope "That All Men Be Saved"?*), and the evangelical pastor and writer Rob Bell (*Love Wins*).

Conversely, the book's last two chapters focus on engagements between Christians and atheists in the here-and-now. Chapter 5 focuses on dialogue. Both inter-religious and inter-denominational dialogue are well-known and uncontroversial features of contemporary Christian practice. Dialogue with unbelievers, however, is far less common – despite the fact that atheists form a sizable and longstanding constituency within western populations. Looking at both historical and contemporary instances of Christian–atheist dialogue, the chapter discusses the 'point' of dialogue, the areas and issues where it is most needed, and how best to go about it. Finally, neither the recognition of atheists' virtues and sincerity, nor the legitimate *hope* for their salvation, countermands the gospel injunction to 'go into all the world and preach the good news to all creation' (Mark 16.16). Central to Chapter 6, therefore, is the importance of mission and evangelization. This argues, among other things, that the evangelistic task facing Christianity in Britain, the USA and elsewhere – sometimes referred to, especially in Catholic circles, as the 'new evangelization' – cannot be limited to apologetics alone, but requires a renewal of the Churches and their members.

To come back to where we started this introduction: St Paul's remark on the Ephesians' erstwhile *atheos*-ity might have little, directly at least, to contribute to a Christian theology of contemporary unbelief. And yet he would, I think, recognize the need for today's Christians to think about and engage with this most striking sign of the times – and to do so humbly, striving sincerely to understand the reasons for and realities of modern atheism, while remaining faithful to those truths and the 'good news' to which Christianity bears witness. This is a small attempt to do just that.

I

The 'atheism' of Christianity

Picture the scene: it's festival day in a provincial Roman city in the mid-second century AD, and people have come from far and wide to witness a group of local Christians being put to death. A young man called Germanicus stands in the arena, not just bravely facing savage beasts but actively urging them on. Irritated by the youth's composure, the crowd who have gathered to see him torn apart cry out: 'Down with the atheists!' Slightly later, the venerable bishop Polycarp is brought into the arena, and is ordered – on pain of death – to himself denounce his fellow Christians in the same way. Whereupon, we are told: 'Polycarp's brow darkened as he threw a look round the turbulent crowd of heathens in the circus; and then, indicating them with a sweep of his hand, he said with a growl and a glance to heaven "Down with the atheists!"' (*Martyrdom of Polycarp*, 9).[1]

St Polycarp, whom ancient tradition assures was a disciple of St John the Evangelist, was bishop of Smyrna (modern-day Izmir on the west coast of Turkey) for much of the first half of the second century. This gripping, eyewitness account of his and his companions' martyrdom around the year 156 is the earliest such report we have, and hence offers invaluable

---

1 The translation here (slightly amended) is taken from Maxwell Staniforth (trans.), 1968, *Early Christian Writings*, Harmondsworth: Penguin, pp. 153–67.

insights into ancient Christian life, thought and practice. For our purposes, the word translated as 'atheists' here is our old friend, *atheoi*. Given the context, its meaning here is rather more transparent than it was in Ephesians. In effect, we have the Christian Polycarp and the pagan crowd mutually denouncing each other as 'infidels'. As far as the crowd is concerned, the Christians deny and dishonour the *real* Roman gods, while affirming their own false one. (At one point, the arena crowd cry out that Polycarp is a 'destroyer of our gods, who is teaching whole multitudes to abstain from sacrificing to them or worshipping them' – *Martyrdom*, 12.) But as far as Polycarp is concerned, the crowd do precisely the opposite.

On one level, this is just an instance of a broad phenomenon noted in the Introduction, of 'atheist' being used throughout much of history as a term of abuse: it is always one's *enemies* who are the 'atheists' (and the feeling is often mutual). However, in the writings of St Justin Martyr, one of Polycarp's contemporaries, the same basic idea receives a somewhat different twist. Justin had himself been brought up a pagan, but in later life, having worked his way through a succession of different philosophies – Stoicism, Pythagoreanism, Aristotelianism and Platonism – he finally settled on Christianity as the 'true Philosophy'. Not incidentally, he was also impressed by the composure and dignity of the Christian martyrs: 'when I was delighting in [hearing] the Christians slandered, and saw them fearless of death, [I] perceived that it was impossible they could be living in wickedness and pleasure' (*Second Apology*, 11).[2]

---

2 This, and all other quotations from Justin's and Pseudo-Justin's (see below) writings, may be found in Alexander Roberts and James Donaldson (eds), 1996, *The Ante-Nicene Fathers, Volume I: The Apostolic Fathers – Justin Martyr – Irenaeus*, Edinburgh: T & T Clark. These and a huge number of other translated texts from the early Church Fathers can also be found at: www.newadvent.org/fathers/.

Roughly a decade after Polycarp met his fate in Smyrna, Justin was himself martyred.

Along with several other second-century Christian thinkers, Justin wrote a number of *apologias* – 'defences' rather than 'apologies' in the usual meaning of the word (and the root of 'apologetics', or the rational defence of Christian doctrine) – in an attempt to explain what and why Christians believed for his pagan contemporaries, and to correct common misunderstandings about them. The charge of 'atheism' was one of these. Justin, however, novelly chooses to side with *both* Polycarp *and* the crowd, declaring in his *First Apology*: 'we confess that we are atheists, so far as gods of this sort [i.e. the Greco-Roman ones] are concerned, but not with respect to the Most True God' (*First Apology*, 6). For Justin then, there is at least one, albeit qualified, sense in which Christians are, and must be, atheists.

Justin is far from alone within the tradition in identifying forms of genuinely *Christian* 'atheism', by which I mean perfectly orthodox forms and varieties of 'atheism' within Christianity. Some of these are stronger than others, but all arguably deserve the name 'atheism', albeit in a subtle and not-to-be-read-naively sort of way (hence inverted commas flag up the genuine, if qualified, deployment of the word).[3] While the rest of this book will concern itself with the theology of what one might call atheism proper (i.e. atheism as the absence of belief in a God or gods, understood in the

---

3 These should not, however, be confused with what one might call forms of 'Christian' *atheism*. I include the various attempts by certain western twentieth-century theologians to affirm the 'death of God' while retaining Christian rituals, language and – often enough – jobs. These fads were, mercifully enough, short-lived. After all, it is rather the point of Christianity that its dead God has a habit of not staying so for very long.

normal way, and hence unadorned by quotation marks), it will be a fruitful and hopefully interesting prelude to consider instead the 'atheism' of proper theology. We will find ourselves in good company: Paul, Justin Martyr, Augustine, Meister Eckhart, Herbert McCabe, John of the Cross and Mother Teresa will all be joining us on our adventure.

God and 'the gods'

The first move for us to make here is to consider more deeply Justin's above quoted remark: 'we confess that we are atheists, so far as gods of this sort are concerned, but not with respect to the Most True God'. Justin's point here is to drive a wedge between the false, so-called 'gods' of the Roman world – e.g. 'we not only deny that they. . . are gods, but assert that they are wicked and impious demons' (*First Apology*, 5) – and the authentic *God* whom Christians proclaim as Lord. This point is made more explicit in another (and perhaps also second-century) text, sometimes ascribed to Justin himself but now considered more likely to be the work of a Justin-inspired disciple. For Pseudo-Justin – as he has come to be known – this 'true and invariable Name' (*On the Sole Government of God*, 6) is only correctly 'applicable to the only true God' (*Government*, 1). Any others given the name, including those whom the pagans *call* gods, receive it unworthily. Hence referring to Greco-Roman mythology, he speaks dismissively of 'those who think that they shall share the holy and perfect Name, which some have received by a vain tradition as if they were gods' (*Government*, 5).

A very similar idea, although expressed slightly differently, appears in the New Testament in 1 Corinthians 8.

4

In the course of giving practical advice on the eating of food sacrificed to idols, Paul also distinguishes between the 'so-called gods in heaven or on earth' and the 'one God' (8.5–6). Paul seems to oscillate between implying that these so-called gods are simple fictions ('no idol in the world really exists') and affirming that though real enough in themselves, these 'many gods and many lords' certainly do not deserve to share the divine name. But regardless of whether they are demons or mere figments, Paul's basic point is clear: 'for us there is one God, the Father, from whom are all things and for whom we exist, and one Lord, Jesus Christ, through whom all things are and through whom we exist' (1 Cor. 8.4–6).

For Paul, as for Justin, Christians must therefore be atheists regarding 'the gods'. And nor is this merely an academic, highfalutinly theological point for him. Rather, he is anxious that the Corinthians be vigilant against lapsing, or inadvertently causing others to lapse, into idolatry – that is, into the offering of worship due to 'the Most True God' to those who are falsely so-called. Recent converts, in particular, might be fooled into thinking that 'the gods', though falsely so-called, are actually deserving of the name: 'Since some have become so accustomed to idols until now, they still think of the food they eat as offered to an idol; and their conscience, being weak, is defiled' (8.7). (Still, hearteningly perhaps, this suggests that crises of catechesis are not a new phenomenon within the Church.) Hence, lest the practice of eating food sacrificed to idols, though in itself innocuous enough, become 'a stumbling-block to the weak', Paul advises against it. Better to go without cheap meat than to confuse others about the distinction between the misnamed 'gods' and the Most – and, for that matter, *only* – True one.

God, falsely so-called

As far as Pseudo-Justin is concerned, the word 'God' is not a description of something but is rather a proper name. For him, the classical gods and goddesses – Zeus, Hera, Hermes, Aphrodite and the rest – are imposters. They are not gods at all but are masquerading under a false name and an assumed identity.

Let us agree with Pseudo-Justin that, for Christians, *God* is first and foremost the name of someone: a someone quite unlike any other someone, it is true, but a someone (or somethree?) nonetheless. Though we may, on occasion, use the word as though it were primarily a description or definition – e.g. 'God, *noun*, an omnipotent, omniscient, omnibenevolent, Creator of the universe' – this does not affect the basic point. Pseudo-Justin assumes, however, that the use of 'God', *theos* in Greek, as a name for the Jews' and Christians' 'Sovereign Lord, who made the heaven and the earth, the sea, and everything in them' (Acts 4.24), somehow precedes the use of 'god' as a description for a class of vastly inferior, supernatural beings domiciled on Mount Olympus. In truth, however, the original borrowing was almost certainly the other way around: Hellenized Jews stealing as a name for Yahweh the already existing Greek descriptive noun *theos*. As such, a converse case can be made for arguing that it is the Judeo-Christian *God* who is falsely, or at least misleadingly, so-called. If so, then Christians 'proclaim ourselves atheists' in a still deeper sense than Justin himself envisages.

This is a point that the twentieth-century Anglo-Irish Dominican theologian Herbert McCabe – a hugely, though subtly, influential figure on much of the best Anglophone theology of the past several decades – was at pains to stress.

To quote a characteristic passage from *God Still Matters*, a posthumous collection of his essays and sermons:

> We do not know what we are talking about when we use the word 'God' . . . When Jews and Christians came to use the word 'god' it was already lying around meaning something else – I mean it meant something that God certainly could not be, a god. Whatever we are referring to when we use the word 'God' it can no more be a god than it can be a model aeroplane or half-past eleven.[4]

This idea is fleshed out more fully in a different essay, slightly earlier in the book:

> 'God', 'Theos', 'Deus' is of course a name borrowed from paganism; we take it out of its proper context, where it is used for talking about the gods, and use it for our own purposes. This is quite a legitimate piece of borrowing and quite safe as long as it does not mislead us into thinking that the God we worship (or don't) is a god . . . He is always dressed verbally in second-hand clothes that don't fit him very well. We always have to be on our guard against taking these clothes as revealing who or what he is.[5]

What McCabe is doing here is effectively turning Pseudo-Justin's argument on its head. He points out that, in its original context, 'god' (*theos*) denotes a class of personal, superhuman, supernatural beings, who collectively possess

---

4 Herbert McCabe, 2002, *God Still Matters*, ed. Brian Davies, London: Continuum, p. 55.

5 McCabe, *God Still Matters*, p. 3.

a wide range of impressive, though limited, super powers. Now, as a *description* of the One worshipped and glorified by the ancient Israelites, and thus latterly the early Christians too, that is a fairly awful one. To give just one example: while Zeus, Hera and Aphrodite may well be very powerful (and vastly more powerful than any human), they are still things *within* the universe. By contrast, the 'God of Abraham, and of Jacob' is considered to be the all-powerful creator and sustainer of the universe *itself*.

But by choosing to refer to this One with the word 'god', Greek-speaking Jews – including, most influentially, those translating the Hebrew Scriptures – were using it as a name, rather than as a literal description. Transferred to this new context, the proper noun *God* became a kind of metaphor. There is a sense in which God is *like* a 'god' (he too is powerful, for example, albeit both far more so, and in a qualitatively different way), just as there is a sense in which God is *like* 'a mighty fortress' (he is steadfast, and protects those who 'dwell within' him). But the Judeo-Christian God cannot be an actual mighty fortress. And he cannot be, as McCabe reminds us, an actual 'god'.

This point may perhaps be more easily grasped if one considers a couple giving their daughter the name of 'Poppy'. They may have many reasons for doing so. Possibly it is a family name, or a tribute to a cantankerous Liverpudlian cat from the children's television of their childhood. It may simply be because they like the sound of the word. Feasibly, however, there is something about *actual* poppies that makes them think it would be a fitting name for a daughter: their beauty, or gracefulness, for example. Perhaps, due to some small but fondly remembered moment in their lives, poppies make the couple smile – and they think this will be true of their Poppy too. They are not, of course, using this word as a straightforward description: she is not, and will not be, an actual member of the botanical family *Papaveraceae*. Instead, the word functions as a kind of metaphor or analogy: by naming her thus, her parents are intimating that they think (or hope) she will be like a poppy *in some way*. Seen objectively, this link may seem somewhat tenuous. There will, after all, be vastly more ways in which the child is not at all like a poppy, than there are ways in which she is: she won't photosynthesize, she won't be a symbol of Remembrance Sunday, she won't be a major ingredient in the production of heroin . . . But nevertheless, there *is* a link, however slight, and one that is, to her parents at least, a significant one.

Naturally, there is no danger whatsoever of anyone in their right mind mistaking this Poppy's metaphorical name for a literal description, as my silly examples above are intended to show. Yet, as McCabe points out, and as Paul and Pseudo-Justin were all too aware, such is not the case with the Christian God. While he may have some points of contact with the Olympian gods, he is not, and could not be, simply a superpowerful 'thing' within the universe: 'Whatever we are referring to when we use the word "God" it can no more be a god than it can be a model aeroplane or half-past eleven.' To think otherwise – to suppose that God is simply a 'god', even if the biggest and best one of them all – is to commit idolatry. And this is, moreover, a point that applies far more widely. Without delving too deeply here into a very fraught and complex area, suffice it to say that it is not just the word 'god' that, if mistaken as a literal description, comes insultingly short. Certainly, a strong case can be made that *all* human words about the Most True God are condemned to be egregiously lacking. Witness, for example, St Augustine's comment on our use of the word 'person' – a stalwart of orthodox trinitarian theology since at least the early third century – as a description for the Father, the Son, and the Holy Spirit:

> Because the Father is not the Son, and the Son is not the Father, and the Holy Spirit . . . is neither the Father nor the Son, then certainly there are three . . . But when it is asked 'Three what?' then the great poverty from which our language suffers becomes apparent. But the formula 'three persons' has been coined, not in order to give a complete explanation by means of it, but in order that we might not be obliged to remain silent. (*On the Trinity*, 5.10)[6]

On arguably similar lines, the thirteenth-century German Dominican theologian Meister Eckhart writes in one of his vernacular sermons: 'let us pray to God that we may be free of God that we may gain the truth and enjoy it eternally.'[7] Quite how this cryptic saying should be understood is a matter of controversy. Eckhart was never one to shy away from verbal pyrotechnics, and his daring and ambiguous phrasing of fundamentally orthodox ideas both landed him in hot water in his own times, and guaranteed him a wildly diverse array of aficionados in subsequent centuries. (Few medieval theologians can claim a list of twentieth-century devotees that is at once so impressive and so dubious as the following: the Marxist philosopher Ernst Bloch, the New Age guru Eckhart Tolle, the Nobel Peace Prize-winning statesman

---

6 Quoted from Gerald O'Collins, 1999, *The Tripersonal God: Understanding and Interpreting the Trinity*, Mahwah, NJ: Paulist Press, p. 141.

7 Quoted from Maurice Walshe (trans.), 2009, *The Complete Mystical Works of Meister Eckhart*, New York: Crossroad, p. 422.

Dag Hammarskjöld, the experimental composer John Cage and the Nazi war criminal Alfred Rosenberg.) One plausible interpretation, however, is that Eckhart is drawing a distinction here between the Most True God ('let us pray to God'), and our flawed human conceptions of who that God actually is ('that we may be free of "god"'), in the interests both of truth and salvation ('that we may gain the truth and enjoy it eternally'). On this reading, Eckhart's utterance is radical enough to be fully orthodox, and a further instance of the kind of theological 'atheism' we have divined in the writings of Paul, Justin, Pseudo-Justin and McCabe. For all of them, the worship of false 'gods' in whatever form – whether Olympian super-things, demons, fictions, or naive theological constructions – amounts to the same: idol worship. Hence in the words of McCabe:

> The worship of [the] Creator is the only worship worthy of a human being . . . This, you might say, was the great Hebrew discovery: human beings are such that they worship *only* the mystery by which there is anything at all instead of nothing . . . [T]he human being is now defined, if you like, as the Creator-worshipper, the atheist with no gods to worship, no gods to petition, no gods to pray to, no gods worth praying to.[8]

'Only an atheist can be a good Christian'

The Marxist philosopher Ernst Bloch, in his rich and remarkable 1972 book *Atheism in Christianity*, famously observed:

---

8 McCabe, *God Still Matters*, p. 56.

'Only an atheist can be a good Christian; only a Christian can be a good atheist.'[9] More recently, the Slovenian intellectual Slavoj Žižek writes: 'not only is *Christianity* (at its core, if disavowed by its institutional practice) *the only truly consistent atheism*, it is also that *atheists are the only true believers*.'[10] Bloch and Žižek are both atheists by our definition, at least in the 'negative' sense of being without a belief in the existence of a God or gods, and the points they are making here are largely political and ethical. For example, Bloch firmly believed that 'the Bible has always been the Church's bad conscience',[11] and he stands out among Marxist theorists for giving due attention to Marx's own observation that the working classes' religious yearnings are, among other things, a *protest* against unjust social conditions. (That's the bit of the 'religion is the opium of the masses' passage that people tend to overlook.) Broadly similar ideas can, however, be found in the works of influential Christian writers also. So far in this chapter we have focused on the 'atheism' of Christianity, albeit in a carefully qualified, subtle, though nonetheless significant, sense of the word: an 'atheism' regarding the 'gods', but not an atheism regarding *God*. The obvious flipside to this is a consideration of the ways in which atheism, and indeed atheists, might have points of contact with these forms of Christian (non)believing.

In the theological literature on atheism, it is possible to identify two main tendencies along these kinds of line. The first is quite negative, and dismisses atheistic ideas and

---

9 Ernst Bloch, 1972, *Atheism in Christianity*, trans. J. T. Swann, New York: Herder & Herder, p. 9.

10 Slavoj Žižek, 2012, *Less Than Nothing: Hegel and the Shadow of Dialectical Materialism*, London: Verso, p. 116 (emphasis in original).

11 Bloch, *Atheism in Christianity*, p. 21.

arguments as being, at best, obvious and platitudinous, and at worst, wholly beside the point. The conceptions of God that atheists deny have, it is claimed, no bearing at all on the God in whom Christians actually believe: such 'so-called gods' are naive and idolatrous caricatures, and Christian thinkers have *already* made short (and rather more sophisticated) work of dismissing them in their strivings to apprehend the Most True God. For example, Denys Turner teases atheists for trumpeting as hard-won conclusions what their theological counterparts take to be nothing more than basic and unremarkable premises:

> [I]n the sense in which atheists of this sort say God 'does not exist', that atheist has merely arrived at the theological starting-point. Theologians of the classical traditions, an Augustine, a Thomas Aquinas or a Meister Eckhart, simply agree about the disposing of idolatries, and then proceed with the proper business of doing theology.[12]

The second tendency, meanwhile, takes the same basic point, but gives it a rather more positive spin. On this view, the atheist is cast as the anti-idolater *par excellence*, rejecting all (mis)conceptions of both God and the gods wholesale, and being, at least for the most part, right to do so: 'atheism properly and effectively criticizes false and misleading images of God'.[13] After all, so this argument sometimes goes, *all* human ideas about God must necessarily fall short of him. This is, as we have seen, the insight of such exemplary Christians thinkers as Augustine and Eckhart. In

---

12 Denys Turner, 2002, *Faith Seeking*, London: SCM Press, p. 8.

13 Étienne Borne, 1961, *Modern Atheism*, trans. S. J. Testier, London: Burns & Oates, p. 144.

its strongest expressions, this strand of Christian thought (sometimes called negative or apophatic theology), as it may be found in the writings of the enigmatic but influential fourth- or fifth-century writer known as Pseudo-Dionysius the Areopagite, asserts that whatever it is that Christians call God, 'It falls neither within the predicate of nonbeing nor of being . . . It is beyond assertion and denial.'[14] And if this is the case, then aren't atheists on to something very profound – and authentically Christian – after all?

Evidence of both these two tendencies occurs in the writings of the Russian novelist Fyodor Dostoevsky. As well as being one of the great geniuses of world literature, Dostoevsky is widely recognized as among the nineteenth century's most profound theological thinkers. His wide-ranging and nuanced engagement with atheism, motivated and informed by his personal grapplings with the subject – he once admitted that his own 'hosanna' had passed through 'a furnace of doubt' – is a case in point. More will be said about it in the following chapter in relation to the problem of suffering and evil. But for our purposes here, note the remark by the saintly Prince Myshkin, the protagonist of Dostoevsky's 1868 novel *The Idiot*, that 'there's something in [true religious feeling] that atheisms eternally glance off, and they will eternally be talking *not about that*.'[15] For Myshkin, atheists are condemned always to 'miss the point' when discussing God and religion: in our terminology, their criticisms of 'god' are irrelevant to

---

14 Quoted from Colm Luibhéid and Paul Rorem (eds and trans.), 1987, *Pseudo-Dionysius: The Complete Works*, Mahwah, NJ: Paulist Press, p. 141.

15 Fyodor Dostoevsky, [1868] 2001, *The Idiot*, trans. Richard Pevear and Larissa Volokhonsky, London: Granta, p. 221.

the Most True one. This is, of course, an instance of the negative, dismissive tendency we noted above.

However, compare the following from a slightly later novel, 1872's *Demons*. Here the Orthodox bishop Tikhon tells the unbeliever Stavrogin: 'A complete atheist stands on the next-to-last upper step to the most complete faith.'[16] Here we see our second tendency in one of its boldest expressions. For Tikhon, the 'complete atheist' is one who has rejected every single false 'god', including everything and anything that takes, or tries to take, the rightful place of the true God (or to quote again the words of Pseudo-Justin: 'those who think that they shall share the holy and perfect Name, which some have received by a vain tradition as if they were gods'). Such a purified position, which Tikhon places higher than all 'incomplete' forms of faith – and thus, one assumes, above the faith of the vast majority of believers, past, present and future – is thus lacking only one thing.

Two things are worth noting here. Tikhon speaks of 'complete' atheism and 'complete' faith, with the presumable implication that very few atheists are so completely, just as very few believers – i.e. the saints – are so completely. The suggestion is, perhaps, that the great majority of atheists aren't as thoroughgoing as they might like to think. Tikhon does not expand upon this point, though the lacuna here may perhaps be supplied by McCabe, for whom a 'false god' is anything in which we mistakenly place our trust and worship:

---

16 Fyodor Dostoevsky, [1872] 2000, *Demons*, trans. Richard Pevear and Larissa Volokhonsky, New York: Everyman: p. 668.

It would be tedious to list the well-known gods of this exceptionally superstitious twentieth century. Quite apart from surviving old ones like astrology, there are a lot of new ones like racism, nationalism, the Market, the Leader . . . you name it.[17]

Also worthy of comment is Tikhon's choice of metaphor. Envisioning the Christian spiritual life as a series of ascending steps, or perhaps ladder rungs, is relatively common, especially in Eastern Orthodoxy. But viewed from this perspective, 'the most complete atheism' isn't simply next-best to the 'most complete faith'. Instead it is a prerequisite for it: a stage that all those seeking complete faith must pass through en route. This is a notion that we shall return to presently.

Both of these tendencies, in Dostoevsky as elsewhere, provide us with considerable food for thought. And at least to some degree, both seem to have something going for them. Regarding the first one, it is surely true that positive atheists often reject specific conceptions of God that, frankly, do not pass muster in classical Christian theology. And regarding the second one, it has been the dominant theme of this chapter that there can indeed be authentically Christian forms of anti-idolatrous 'atheism'. But – at least in their bolder and least qualified expressions – both tendencies arguably tell us far more about Christian theology than they do about actual atheists. Regarding the former, let us accept that most unbelievers aren't especially well acquainted with the minutiae of the Christian doctrine of God. The same is unquestionably true of a great many pious, practising, faith-*and*-works Christian believers.

---

17 McCabe, *God Still Matters*, p. 32.

Theologians are, needless to say, rather slower off the mark to deride the conceptions of God in which they (explicitly) believe, or think they do, than they are to do the same to the conceptions of God in which many atheists do not. Let us note, too, an idea that will be a major theme of Chapter 3: if the typical discourse about God really is so woefully ill-informed, then is that not at least partly the fault of Christians themselves?

Furthermore, while there may well be a certain correlation between atheism and negative theology (and one that we have been gleefully exploiting in this chapter), it is surely rather a stretch to identify the two too closely. For all of McCabe's and Justin's legitimate distinction between *God* and 'the gods', and for all of Pseudo-Dionysius' awareness of the difficulties of trying to say something about this reality that doesn't fall infinitely and insultingly short of it, the fact remains that, unlike atheists, Christians do indeed affirm the existence of God – and a God whose name, howsoever metaphorically and requiring of qualification, does indeed convey at least something of significance about him (just as Poppy's name does of her). So while it is true to say that there is a sense in which Christians are indeed 'atheists' (regarding mere 'gods'), it does not follow conversely that all unbelievers are but apophatic theologians of a Pseudo-Dionysian bent. For they, atheists *sans* inverted commas, are without a belief in the existence, not only of gods but of the Most True God as well.

'The deeper the darkness'

So far in this chapter, we have focused on what one could call intellectual or theological types of 'atheism' in Christianity:

insistences that, one way or another, Christians worship 'the God who is not a god'.[18] However, there is another, and arguably more significant, kind within the Christian tradition: the experiential 'atheism' of some of the mystics. As before, the word is used here in a sense rather different from atheism's usual one. Yet there is enough contact between the normal meaning, and our heavily qualified, 'inverted-commas' usage, to justify the calculated risk of serious misunderstanding. It need hardly be said that John of the Cross, Mother Teresa, Padre Pio and even Jesus himself – all figures to whom we shall refer below – were not atheists in the term's normal meaning. Nevertheless, the experiences of 'godforsakenness' that all underwent – while, it should be stressed, wholly foreign to the vast majority of normal atheists – are certainly worthy of comment in a chapter with a title such as this. This is, however, a huge topic in its own right: *The Absence of God in the Lives of the Saints* would make for a very fine, though very long, book. As such, only some brief remarks are possible here.

According to the Gospels, Christ cried out from the Cross the opening lines of Psalm 22: 'My God, my God, why have you forsaken me?' (Mark 15.31). In the words' original context, the Psalmist's despair leads on to an affirmation of the Lord's victorious constancy. Within the wider context of Easter, the same is true here as well. But that need not mean, on that particular Friday afternoon, that Jesus intended them with anything less than full sincerity. By the medieval period, these crucial words of Christ's came to be deeply significant among Christian mystics identifying with the sufferings of the Cross. In the medieval period, for example, influential figures such as Blessed Angela of Foligno

---

18 McCabe, *God Still Matters*, p. 32.

(1248–1309), St Mechthild of Magdeburg (*c.* 1210–*c.* 1285) and Blessed Margaret Ebner (1291–1351) reported periods of feeling abandoned by God. Quoting the latter's experience, for instance: 'my Lord Jesus Christ placed me in such indescribable misery and a feeling of abandonment that it seemed as if I had never experienced the grace of our Lord in my whole life. I had completely lost trust in his mercy.'[19] Two and a half centuries later, such episodes would receive their classic crystallization as 'the dark night of the soul' of the Spanish poet-theologian St John of the Cross:

> When this purgative contemplation oppresses a man, he feels very vividly indeed the shadow of death, the sighs of death, and the sorrows of hell, all of which reflect the feeling of God's absence, of being chastised and rejected by Him, and of being unworthy of Him, as well as the object of his anger. The soul experiences all this and even more, for now it seems that this affliction will last forever.[20]

Without supposing them all to be the same in either nature or source, experiences like these have been reported by many leading figures in the Christian tradition (as well as by a great many other people, Christians and not too). Witness the Italian stigmatist Padre Pio, for example, writing in 1918:

---

19 Quoted in Bernard McGinn, 1998, *The Flowering of Mysticism: Men and Women in the New Mysticism (1200–1350)*, New York: Crossroad Herder, p. 241.

20 Kieran Kavanaugh and Otilio Rodriguez (eds and trans.), 1966, *The Collected Works of St. John of the Cross*, London: Thomas Nelson, p. 338.

I keep my eyes fixed on the East in the night which surrounds me, to discover that miraculous star which guided our forebears to the Grotto of Bethlehem. But I strain my eyes in vain to see that luminary rise in the heavens . . . The more I fix my gaze the dimmer my sight becomes . . . the deeper the darkness which envelopes me. I am alone by day and night and no ray of light comes through to enlighten me.[21]

Dostoevsky, too, seems not to have been a stranger to such episodes. When viewing Hans Holbein's *Dead Christ in the Tomb* – a full-size, horizontal painting of his wounded and rigor-mortising cadaver – at the gallery in Basel, his wife reports that he stood transfixed, and seemed on the verge of an epileptic seizure.[22] And to these we might also add the Catholic saints Thérèse of Lisieux, Paul of the Cross and Gemma Galgani.

John of the Cross aside, perhaps the most famous sufferer of such spiritual desolation is Mother Teresa of Calcutta, foundress of the Missionaries of Charity and recipient of the Nobel Prize for Peace in 1979. Her 40 years of near-constant 'darkness', thirsting for the God who had once felt so near (and sometimes, rarely and fleetingly, did still), were only fully revealed with the publication of her private writings in 2007. Among the many, harrowing descriptions she gives of it, the following is perhaps the most detailed (with her own distinctive punctuation style intact):

---

21 Quoted in C. Bernard Ruffin, 1991, *Padre Pio: The True Story*, Huntington, IN: Our Sunday Visitor, pp. 149–50.

22 See Malcolm Muggeridge, 2011, *The Gospel in Dostoyevsky: Selections from his Writings*, Rifton, NY: Plough, pp. vi–vii.

Darkness is such that I really do not see – neither with my mind nor with my reason. – The place of God in my soul is blank. – There is no God in me. – When the pain of longing is so great – I just long & long for God – and then it is that I feel – He does not want me – He is not there . . . Sometimes – I just hear my own heart cry out –'My God' and nothing else comes. – The torture and pain I can't explain . . . I long for God – I want to love Him – to love Him much – to live only for love of Him – to love only – and yet there is but pain – longing and no love.[23]

Given statements such as these, it is not at all surprising that Teresa's revelations were widely interpreted as proof of her having been an atheist, pure and simple (and thus, naturally, a hypocrite). But, of course, things are not nearly so simple. While one can indeed speak here of an *experiential* 'atheism' – the 'atheism' of one who acutely, and painfully, perceives God's seeming absence – this is plainly not atheism in any simple or straightforward sense of the word. In the above quotation, apparently atheistic statements are set alongside, and hence qualified by, expressions of abiding trust and abandonment to the One who seems so absent. This is even clearer in those statements of her darkness that are, unmistakably, written as prayers. Consider, for example:

So many unanswered questions live within me – I am afraid to uncover them – because of the blasphemy . . .

23 Quoted in Brian Kolodiejchuk (ed.), 2008, *Mother Teresa: Come Be My Light: The Revealing Private Writings of the Nobel Peace Prize Winner*, London: Rider, p. 210.

When I try to raise my thoughts to Heaven – there is such convicting emptiness that those very thoughts return like sharp knives & hurt my soul . . . If this brings You glory, if You get a drop of joy from this – if souls are brought to You – if my suffering satiates Your Thirst – here I am Lord, with joy I accept all to the end of life – & I will smile at Your Hidden Face – always.[24]

Just as Justin's affirmation of the Most True God qualifies and explains his acceptance of the label 'atheist', so too do Teresa's *prayers* concerning her lack of faith undermine any identification of her as an actual atheist. (Except in our duly qualified and orthodox sense of the word.) And as with other figures in the Christian tradition, it was precisely Teresa's feeling of abandonment that proved the catalyst for her ever-deepening faith in, and service to, Christ. The two hallmarks of her spirituality, devotion to the Eucharist and devotion to the destitute, stem from her longing to be in Christ's presence. Taking Scripture at its word on both counts – 'This is my body' (Mark 14.22) and 'Just as you did it to one of the least of my brother, you did it to me' (Matt. 25.40) – she sought to fill the void of his absence at the level of her felt experience. In a rather different, but no less significant, way from Justin, she thus sought and found the Most True God.

Conclusion

The purpose of this opening chapter was intentionally provocative: to show the ways in which 'atheism' – although

24 Kolodiejchuk, pp. 187–8.

not atheism in the normal sense – sits close to the heart of classical Christian theology and spirituality. To a certain degree, this helps us to see some of the points of constructive contact between faith and unbelief. For example, atheists' critiques can indeed aid us in purifying our ever-faulty notions of 'the God who is not a god'. But it should also help us to guard against naive claims as to the alleged affinities between genuine atheism and authentic Christianity. It will be an abiding theme of this book that the difference between faith and unbelief – between following, howsoever falteringly, the Most True God, and not – is indeed one of mighty significance.

2

Reasons to disbelieve

'Fools say in their hearts, "There is no God".' This opening line from Psalms 14 and 53 – curiously, the two are almost identical – is sometimes taken as proof that atheism was a recognized, if maligned, position in ancient Hebrew society. Closer inspection, however, reveals that this may not be the case: both psalms are actually devoted to denouncing, not unbelief itself but widespread immorality (e.g. 'They have all fallen away, they are all alike perverse; there is no one who does good, no, not one' – Ps 14.3; Ps 53.3). This would, then, be 'godlessness' in the pejorative ethical sense that we have previously encountered also in classical Greek. And certainly, the consensus of the rabbinical commentators was that the Psalmist's 'fools' are those who contradict their own affirmation *in theory* of the first four of the Ten Commandments (relating to YHWH), through their failure *in practice* to uphold the final six (relating to their neighbours). This was likewise the majority report of the early Christian commentators, who similarly took 'say *in their hearts*' to imply that the Psalmist's targets are not those who either openly avow ('say'), or even think to themselves ('say in their heads'), 'there is no God' in any speculative or intellectual sense.[1]

---

1 See Mark J. Edwards, 2013, 'The First Millennium', in Stephen Bullivant and Michael Ruse (eds), *The Oxford Handbook of Atheism*, Oxford: Oxford University Press.

Regardless of these psalms' actual subjects, it is clear enough today that it is neither only nor predominantly fools who say, 'There is no God.' Evidently there are huge numbers of intelligent, educated, reasonable people who are atheists in either the positive or negative sense. Some of these are high-profile, public figures, including natural scientists, philosophers, social scientists, journalists, novelists, politicians, bloggers, artists and stand-up comedians. But the vast majority are just, well, 'ordinary' people; ordinary in the sense of being one's everyday friends, family, colleagues and acquaintances (each of whom is, however, extraordinary in his or her own way). These are not, by and large, people who write, talk or think about atheism in any regular or systematic manner. They may never even have reflected upon why (or even that) they don't believe in the existence of a God or gods, and if pressed, might not be able to give a particularly coherent or compelling account. But they are, however, far from being fools. Statistically speaking, globally there is a clear, positive correlation between education and unbelief, such that, in general terms, the better educated a person is, the more likely it is that he or she does not believe in God(s).[2] It is worth

---

2 According to the 1999–2004 World Values Survey, collating data from 66 different countries, non-believers made up 10.3% of those with a 'lower' (primary) level of educational attainment, 15.1% of those with a 'middle' (secondary) level, and 15% of those with an 'upper' (tertiary) level. This disproportionate presence of atheists among the well educated is, naturally, prima facie evidence for unbelief's general reasonableness. That said, complex social factors are indubitably also accountable. Those naively attempting to read from these statistics a demonstration of the 'truth' of atheism might like to consider that the WVS records an even stronger, positive correlation between educational attainment and belief in telepathy. The WVS's database is freely available at: www.worldvaluessurvey.org.

nothing, however, that even very wise people are perfectly capable of believing foolish things about certain topics.

There are, it must be said, a great many different sorts of 'reasons' why a person may either not believe in the existence of a God or gods ('negative atheism'), or have a definite belief in his/their non-existence ('positive atheism'). Some of the strongest and most significant of these are not intellectual at all but social and cultural. This is a point that is frequently overlooked, not least by atheists themselves. Fairly frequently, for example, the genuine social and cultural influences on *religious* believing are cited to show that religious views cannot *really* be held for rational reasons. Often the argument goes something like this: people born in Israel are most likely to believe that Judaism is the true religion; people in the Philippines, Catholic Christianity; in Saudi Arabia, Islam; and so on. But if (it continues) one's religious convictions are so obviously influenced by where one is born, then surely people's choices can't be based on an objective and rational evaluation of facts. Sometimes this point is then followed up with the pithy, despairing remark of Jonathan Swift: 'It is useless to attempt to reason a man out of a thing he was never reasoned into.'

Such an argument is, however, highly misleading. It is certainly true that family, upbringing, environment – indeed a whole host of social factors – profoundly influence our religious beliefs. That is not to say that nobody who is brought up by Hindu parents in a Hindu way in a Hindu country ever decides, later in life, to give it all up and become (say) a Scientologist. But such people are, in terms of social trends (and no doubt in several other ways too), exceptional. The bottom line is that social and cultural factors affect pretty well *all* our beliefs. Politically active parents produce disproportionate numbers of politically active children. People brought up in countries where corporal punishment is considered acceptable are more likely to accept it themselves. And furthermore, there is very strong evidence to show that being an unbeliever is likewise powerfully influenced by such mundane, non-intellectual factors as the religious practice and belief of one's parents, the society in which one grew up, the friends one has, and so on.

That is not to imply that because there are these social influences, then unbelief may be written off as just another arational belief stance ('it is useless to attempt to reason a man out of a thing . . .' and all that). But it is important to note that intellectual ideas and arguments are never heard, received, interpreted, rejected or accepted within a socio-cultural vacuum. This is a point that shall be developed further in Chapters 3 ('Is it not our own fault?') and 6 ('New Evangelization?'). In this chapter, though, we will broach a small number of key, intellectual reasons that atheists commonly have or give for their unbelief. More specifically, I wish to focus on some that are directly relevant to Christianity. Rejecting Christianity is not the same thing at all as accepting atheism (whether by conscious decision or default). Nevertheless, in our western context the two frequently go hand in hand. I claim no real interest in these pages in defending or discussing 'religion' or 'theism' as generic phenomena. This book is titled *Faith and Unbelief*, and while the second noun does indeed properly refer to any and all 'God or gods', the first one does not. Rather, it is the highly specific faith in 'Jesus Christ, and him crucified' (1 Cor. 2.2); a faith that entails a rejection of *all the gods* – bar, that is, the Most True one. In what follows, I will not be making any great attempt to rebut these reasons to disbelieve: important though works of apologetics are, this is not one of them. My primary purpose here is understanding, rather than refutation. As such, we will consider a few of the key reasons why so many people today, wise ones and fools alike, find the existence of (the Christian) God to be so implausible. These are: the scandalous nature of the Christian proclamation itself; the problem of suffering and evil; and the perceived all-sufficiency of science. Secondarily, and by necessity somewhat cursorily, I would like to situate these – in many cases, perfectly reasonable – objections within a properly theological context.

'Foolishness to Gentiles'

The Most True God is, it must be acknowledged from the off, an extraordinarily odd kind of being (if, that is, he is a 'being' at all). And the followers of this God subscribe to – or say they do – a list of quite ludicrous-seeming propositions.

It is one thing to affirm a God who is all-powerful, all-knowing and all-loving, who created and sustains 'all things visible and invisible'. That, in itself, is a fairly striking and radical claim; one that, in its time, was revolutionary in human history and that the infant Christianity imbibed at the breast of Judaism. But it is quite another thing to claim that this Creator God – or worse, one of three 'persons' of this *one* God – 'took flesh', resulting in a *someone* both fully God and fully human. Consider, for example, probably the two most instantly recognizable – and thus the most easily ignorable – symbols of Christianity: the baby Jesus and the Cross or Crucifix. The first of these proclaims that this God-man spent a significant amount of time doing things like suffering from colic and cradle cap, screaming in the night for no discernible reason, and weeing incontinently over his sleep-deprived (human) parents. Tears, tantrums and teething are thus the works of the Most True God, just as surely as are 'the heaven and the earth, the sea, and everything in them' (Acts 4.24). The second of these proclaims that the God-man was tortured and murdered; subjected not even to some grandiosely 'superlative' mode of suffering and death as might befit a King, but merely to the tawdrily mundane form of execution to which the Roman Empire treated countless slaves, pirates and enemies of the state (which, in itself, begs an interesting question about the kind of God this Most True one is).

It is perhaps fair to say that most believers do not quite realize the outrageous character of these most basic and taken-for-granted hallmarks of Christianity. (Surely there is something at least a little strange about hanging around one's neck a miniature corpse nailed to a tiny cross?) Irrespective of whether they are true or not, these are surely among the wildest and most monstrous claims ever proposed in human history. And if they are true, then they are, or ought to be, the most profound and world-inverting facts about life and the universe. Yet somehow, in the course of nearly two thousand years, these claims have become so familiar, so tamed and domesticated, as to seem hardly worthy of comment, let alone wonder or puzzlement, among the great majority of those who profess them.

Such was not, however, the case for those to whom the good news of Jesus Christ was first proposed. As Paul famously put it: 'we proclaim Christ crucified, a stumbling-block to Jews and foolishness to Gentiles' (1 Cor. 1.23). For the Jews, of course, the claim that the Messiah, whether God himself or not, had come but had been crucified was blasphemously scandalous (skandalon being Greek for 'stumbling-block'). And they were, it should be said, perfectly reasonable in thinking so: *nobody* was expecting a crucified-and-raised Messiah (hence Peter's 'satanic' rebuke to Jesus in Matthew 16, and the disappointment of those trudging away from Jerusalem on Easter morning regarding him who they '*had hoped* . . . would be the one to redeem Israel' in Luke 24). For the Gentiles, meanwhile, the entire proclamation was manifest folly. The very idea that the *King* of the Jews – indeed, of the whole world – would hail not merely from a backwater of the Empire (Judea) but from of a backwater of that backwater (Galilee); would arrive on donkeyback as the leader of a motley assemblage of peasants and fishermen; and would be arrested and crucified as a common criminal, before miraculously coming back to life a few days later as the saviour of the world – surely these were the ravings, as the second-century pagan writer Celsus put it, of 'women, slaves, and little children'.[3]

For those who have been brought up with this narrative, and with the idea of a God who was truly a human being – however imperfectly or infrequently expressed or reflected upon – it is very hard indeed to be genuinely confronted with the Christian proclamation in all of its (apparently) scandalous foolishness. It is very easy to nod along, half-heartedly (a Creator who is a baby . . . *fine*; a God who gets murdered . . . *sure*; a carpenter who saves the universe . . . *so what else is new?*) as though these were the most boringly obvious platitudes one has ever heard. And, it has to be said, all too often Christian preaching and apologetics – presenting 'Christ, and him crucified' as something self-evident and uncontroversial, to which all right-minded, unobtuse people should naturally and unproblematically assent – reinforces

---

3 Quoted in Ramsay McMullen, 1984, *Christianizing the Roman Empire, A.D. 100–400*, New Haven, CT: Yale University Press, p. 37.

this view. But as more and more people are brought up apart from these narratives, and as what one might call casual, cultural Christianity declines still further (nativity scenes in town squares, crosses in public, prayers in state-school assemblies), it is no surprise that for many the basic claims of Christianity are beginning to seem stranger and stranger. And they have, it must be said, a very good point.

Reactions of incredulity, and even of ridicule, to the Christian message are ultimately misguided. But given the very nature of that message, they are perhaps not unreasonable ones. The fact is that what Christianity proposes is something genuinely radical and subversive, and as such *ought* to require a significant degree of getting one's head around it. (I am reminded here of some of the wholly outlandish – though, I have no doubt, perfectly true – revelations of modern physics: that the *vast* majority of matter is empty space; that there are perhaps as many as 400 *billion* solar systems in the Milky Way, and that this is only one of over 100 *billion* galaxies in the observable universe as a whole. These, too, are propositions that we tend to nod along to, but how difficult they are truly to take on board.) The fact that scepticism can be a reasonable response to the Christian conviction does not mean that it is in any way the correct one, or – very significantly – that it is either the *only* or the *most* reasonable reaction. Christ's own disciples, however, were not beyond admitting 'This teaching is difficult; who can accept it?' (John 6.60). And indeed, in the Gospels they fail time and again to grasp the full import of who Christ is and what this signifies (e.g. Mark 8.14–21). In thinking about the Christian engagement with modern unbelief – not least with the recent growth of mocking and ridiculing forms – we will perhaps do well to bear this fact in mind.

'The rock of atheism'

The Swiss theologian Hans Küng once described the existence and extent of suffering in the world as 'the rock of atheism'.[4] He is surely right. All too often and all too much, human beings, in common with many other types of animal, appear to inhabit what the Latin hymn *Salve Regina* plausibly dubs a 'valley of tears'. Life's trials – ranging from dull, daily pains and sorrows, to truly horrendous instances of catastrophe or depravity – are familiar enough to all that we need not dwell here on examples and illustrations. And such times of trouble and tragedy, our own and those of others, present searing challenges to the very notion of an all-powerful and all-loving 'sovereign Lord' of it all.

In the philosophy of religion this is usually known as the problem of evil. There are many formal statements of the problem, all with their own nuances and subtleties, but the common thread is one that presents itself automatically to most people when hearing the news of some colossal disaster, whether a tsunami, a school shooting, a suicide or a stillbirth: *If* there is a God, then how could it allow such a thing to happen? All statements of the 'problem' are but variations on this theme, and the more that philosophized expressions of it abstract from concrete instances of suffering and evil, the more they lose their compelling, existential power. Suffering in the abstract is far easier to reconcile with an equally abstractly conceived divinity of goodness and power. Such reconciliations are the stock in trade of *theodicy*, the attempt to demonstrate the justice (*dikē*) of God (*theos*) in the face of suffering and evil. This is not

---

4 Hans Küng, 1976, *On Being a Christian*, trans. Edward Quinn, Garden City, NY: Doubleday, p. 432.

the place to survey such attempts, however, since even if successful in theory, they too lose their force when arrayed against the actual tragedies to which human beings are subject: the Augustinian Free Will defence, essentially correct though it may be, is scant comfort to motherless child and childless mother alike.

Undoubtedly the most famous, and indeed most persuasive, expression of the problem of evil – and thus probably the most convincing case for positive atheism – in all of western literature gains its power from precisely this fact. This occurs in the chapter titled 'Rebellion' in Dostoevsky's 1880 novel *The Brothers Karamazov*. In itself, that fact is worthy of some comment: as we saw in the last chapter, Dostoevsky was himself no atheist. Moreover, it was his express intention in writing the novel 'to depict the extreme of blasphemy and the core of the destructive idea of our age . . . and, along with the blasphemy and anarchism, the refutation of them'.[5] Never a creator of straw men, however, Dostoevsky thus supplies the intellectual Ivan with an argument that he himself considered irresistible.

Speaking in a pub to his younger brother, the novice monk Alyosha, Ivan confides that he has a hobby of collecting 'certain kinds of little anecdotes' out of newspapers, detailing horrors done to children. The principal thrust of Ivan's indictment of God simply consists in a litany of some of these, most adapted from real life. (Significantly, Dostoevsky filled his own diaries and notebooks with such press clippings.) These include soldiers bayoneting babies before their mothers' eyes, a five-year-old girl locked in an outdoor latrine all night in winter and a young serf-boy

---

5 Quoted in Jessie Coulson, 1962, *Dostoevsky: A Self-Portrait*, London: Oxford University Press, pp. 219–20.

torn to shreds by a pack of dogs for injuring the foot of the landowner's favourite hound. While Ivan accepts that an omnipotent God can indeed create 'some future harmony' where 'every tear is wiped away' (cf. Rev. 21.4), the thrust of his rebellion is that he nevertheless refuses to be complicit in such a system, however well it might all turn out.

> Is there in the whole world a being who could and would have the right to forgive? I don't want harmony, for love of mankind I don't want it. I want to remain with unrequited suffering. I'd rather remain with my unrequited suffering and my unquenched indignation, *even if I am wrong*. Besides, they have put too high a price on harmony; we can't afford to pay so much for admission. And therefore I hasten to return my entrance ticket . . . It's not that I don't accept God, Alyosha, I just most respectfully return him the ticket.[6]

Carried along by the unrelenting force of Ivan's argument, as every reader of Dostoevsky's work is surely bound to be, the pious Alyosha's instant reaction is to accept his brother's conclusion. He further agrees that, were he positioned as the architect of human history, even one tortured child is too great a price no matter what future, genuinely joyful edifice might be built on its foundation. In the terms of the argument set out by Ivan, moreover, he is surely right.

Yet missing from Ivan's picture, as Alyosha instantly realizes, is any mention of Christ:

---

6 Fyodor Dostoevsky, [1880] 2004, *The Brothers Karamazov*, trans. Richard Pevear and Larissa Volokhonsky, London: Vintage, p. 245 (emphasis in original).

[Y]ou asked just now, is there is in the whole world a being who could and would have the right to forgive? But there is such a being and he can forgive everything, forgive *and for all*, because he himself gave his innocent blood for all and for everything. You've forgotten about him, but it is on Him that the structure is being built, and it is to him that they will cry out, 'Just are thou, O Lord, for thy ways have been revealed!'[7]

Now, the *specific* argument that Alyosha is making here is never properly revealed, as Ivan veers off at this prompting into his equally famous 'Legend of the Grand Inquisitor', which he believes nullifies Alyosha's objection (although readers of the text have long disputed whether, and how, it is meant to do this – and Alyosha takes it as supporting his own point, rather than contradicting it). Certainly, such a cursory appeal to Christ in itself here hardly undercuts the entirety of Ivan's disquisition. And furthermore, it is not my intention here to 'show why Ivan is wrong' or even to try to. Nevertheless, Alyosha's objection shifts the focus considerably, and situates the problem of evil precisely in its properly theological context.

The point to be made here is, in fact, fairly simple. The great bulk of statements of the problem of evil (Ivan's included), and a good number of even the Christian responses to it, ignore Christ entirely. Implicit within Ivan's rebellion is the notion of God as an aloofly remote 'architect', fashioning human history from the perspective of an unaffected outsider. Theodicy-builders, too, typically answer the cry of 'Why do bad things happen to good and innocent people?' by constructing justifications for why a generically omnipotent,

---

7 Dostoevsky, *Brothers Karamazov*, p. 246 (emphasis in original).

omnibenevolent and omniscient 'God' might allow them (e.g. out of respect for the greater good of the autonomy of human beings' free will, and/or being constrained by the utility of a regularly functioning natural order). This is not in any way to denigrate these endeavours, which are valuable and important. However, from a Christian perspective, it can hardly be said that an off-the-peg 'God of classical theism' is functionally equivalent to the Most True one. The philosophers' map, like so many others, is not the terrain, and without due recognition of this fact, discussers of the problem of evil on both sides – again to quote another of Dostoevsky's creations – 'will eternally be talking *not about that*' (emphasis in original).

If we take the Gospels seriously, then the sheer fact that horrendously bad things happen to the good and innocent is not merely unsurprising but is rather the founding principle of the Christian message: 'Jesus Christ, and him crucified' (1 Cor. 2.2). It is common enough to hear Christianity 'explained away' as the product of infantile, wishful thinking; a comfort-blanket for people unable to accept the harsh realities of the world. That is, though, a strange judgement to make of a belief-system whose primary comment on human history is: *even God gets murdered*. Or rather, as Terry Eagleton has perceptively written, 'The crucifixion proclaims that the truth of human history is a tortured political criminal.'[8] In the Gospels Christ also makes plain that not only must 'he undergo great suffering' (Matt. 16.21) but further that: 'If any want to become my followers, let them deny themselves and take up their cross and follow me. For those who want to save their life will lose it, and those who

---

8 Terry Eagleton, 2007, 'Introduction', in Terry Eagleton and Giles Fraser (eds), *Jesus Christ: The Gospels*, London: Verso, p. xxvii.

lose their life for my sake will find it' (16.24–25). His earliest
followers, of course, were no strangers to this fact. And nor,
considered in global terms, are his more recent disciples any
the less cognizant: there are said to have been many times
more martyrs for Christianity in the twentieth century than
in *all* the previous centuries put together. In the sobering
and uncomfortable words of Oscar Romero, the Catholic
Archbishop of San Salvador who was shot down while cel-
ebrating Mass in 1980: 'A Church that does not suffer per-
secution should fear for itself. It is not the true Church of
Jesus Christ.'[9]

Such reflections do not, of course, dissolve away the problem of evil. If anything, they make it deeper and darker still.
Nevertheless, it is surely the case that any Christian answer
to the problem of evil must, first of all, be framed against the
background of a God who becomes not only a real human
being but one who, in solidarity with countless billions of
his fellow human beings, 'was despised and rejected by others; a man of suffering and acquainted with infirmity; and as
one from whom others hide their faces he was despised, and
we held him of no account' (Isaiah 53.3; cf. Phil. 2.6–8).
This is, moreover, a God who does not spare even his own
dearest followers (including the apostles and innumerable
saints, known and unknown, down through the ages) from
a similar fate. Hence whatever ultimate reasons there might
be for an omnipotent, omniscient and omnibenevolent
God to allow such evils as there are in the world, he cannot be accused of exempting either himself, in Christ, or
his friends, from full exposure to the awful – if ultimately
justified – consequences. Nor, incidentally, can we accuse

---

9 Quoted in Jon Sobrino, 2008, *No Salvation Outside the Poor:
Prophetic-Utopian Essays*, New York: Orbis, pp. 93–4.

Christ of being stoically blasé about human suffering and death, whether his own (e.g. his agony in Gethsemane and his previously discussed 'cry of desolation') or those of others (e.g. his weeping at the death of Lazarus; his compassion for the afflicted throughout the Gospels). Second of all, it must also be apprehended in light of a God who, having accepted that evil and suffering are (for whatever reason) endemic to human existence, nevertheless *overcomes* and *overturns* them on Easter morning. Importantly, this is done in way that does not simply 'erase', 'reverse' or 'blot out' past sufferings, since Christ retains his wounds even after the resurrection. Indeed, it is salutary to note that it is *precisely* these wounds, the marks of his suffering and death, that remain, while the rest of his appearance seems to have altered beyond recognition – so much so that his closest associates struggle to identify him (e.g. Luke 24.36–40, 25.13–32; John 20.11–16, 21.1–7).

Again, this theological (or rather *christological*) context far from 'solves' the problem of evil, which remains as ever it will the keenest and most challenging objection to Christian believing, and most especially at the immediate, concrete and existential level (as opposed to the abstract and theoretical level, though it is powerful here too). But then it was never meant to. If, however, Christianity can offer an adequate answer to Ivan Karamazov, then his brother is quite right that it must begin and end with the crucified and risen one. As the American author Addison Hodges Hart puts it, in his provocative and compelling book *Knowing Darkness*:

> The cross of Christ is especially shocking because it's not a religious answer at all, but a divine answer that is luridly profane in nature. An instrument of torture and capital punishment, reserved for the slaves and dregs of

human society, becomes the means of salvation right here 'under the sun' – and in fact the sun itself is darkened by it.[10]

All things, visible and invisible?

There is a widespread perception, common to atheists and believers alike, that atheism and science are, in some way, intrinsically linked. Strictly speaking this is not inevitable: an absence of belief in the existence of a God or gods in itself implies nothing whatsoever about science and is perfectly compatible with all manner of beliefs and opinions in this general area, as in just about any other. On our definition, for instance, there is nothing to stop an atheist, qua atheist, from believing in angels, sprites, ghosts, or leprechauns, or that the earth is flat or that fossils and the moon landing are part of a vast, government conspiracy.

That said, this perceived connection is undoubtedly a real one. A great many positive atheists cite 'science' – either in general or some specific finding or theory – as one of the main justifications for their position, and unbelief is frequently accompanied by a naturalistic and/or materialistic world view of one sort or another. *Some* atheists would go so far as to claim that, at root, 'being (properly) scientific' and 'being (properly) religious' are incompatible: a conviction that might manifest itself in assertions that eminent scientists who claim to hold theological beliefs cannot *really*

---

10 Addison Hodges Hart, 2009, *Knowing Darkness: On Skepticism, Melancholy, Friendship, and God*, Grand Rapids, MI: Eerdmans, pp. 69–70.

do so.[11] Views this strong (not to mention unlikely), however, are relatively uncommon. In general, however, there is a widespread view that, at best, 'science' and 'religion' make uneasy bedfellows, and that even if science doesn't necessarily *demand* positive atheism, modern science has seriously undermined whatever plausibility religious world views, of whatever kind, might once have had in less enlightened times. Given the significance of this kind of belief, and its taken-for-granted status (including among many Christians), it will be worth our making a few brief comments here.

This is, however, neither the time not place for a detailed rundown of the relationship between 'religion' and 'science' – not least because there is no single, coherent thing that either of those nouns picks out. Both refer, in very general terms, to amorphous and diffuse millennia-old spheres of human interest and endeavour, success and failure, and enlightenment and obfuscation. Even confining oneself to the modern, western, post-Renaissance scientific tradition on the one hand, and mainstream European Christianity on the other, one is dealing with a huge and tangled web of concords, conflicts and contradictions. One is therefore well-advised to be wary of any too-easy generalizations.

It is true enough that the Churches have, on occasion, condemned not just certain scientific theories but also those who have proposed or propagated them, and that they have sometimes done so in an intensely regrettable way. Certain names spring immediately to mind in this connection – e.g. Galileo Galilei and Giordano Bruno – and while the actual history is inevitably more complex than later caricatures, these are scarcely among the more glorious chapters in the

---

11 E.g. Richard Dawkins, 2006, *The God Delusion*, London: Bantam Press, pp. 152–3.

history of Christianity. Nevertheless, it remains difficult to read out of these any Christian animus against 'science in general'. In almost all such cases, what one is witnessing is the Church expressing its support, however ill-advisedly, in favour of one scientific theory or group of scientists against a different theory and/or group. Thus while it is easy enough, in retrospect, to lambaste Pope Urban VIII for reprimanding Galileo, it is convenient to forget that the genius scientist's sun-centred model of the cosmos was opposed by the overwhelming consensus of *other scientists* too.

Something similar is true of another celebrated moment in the 'science-versus-religion conflict': Christopher Columbus' failure to convince the scholars assembled at Salamanca to support his bid to sail westwards to the Indies. While popular myth locates the disagreement in Columbus' maintaining, in the alleged face of religious ignorance, that the Earth was round, this is not so. No scholar seriously doubted the Earth's sphericity (nor had they, with just one or two minor exceptions, throughout the whole course of Christian history). The cleric-scholars of Salamanca did, though, affirm the established, mainstream scientific opinion that it was a sphere of roughly twice the size that Columbus supposed. As such, they doubted his ships could carry sufficient supplies to get them as far as the Indies. And this time, unlike in the Galileo affair, the Church (albeit, in this case, an unofficial panel of priests and scholars) was absolutely right. Had Columbus not chanced upon the Americas – although he himself never realized quite what he had discovered – then the *Niña*, the *Santa María* and the *Pinta* would never have been seen again.[12]

---

12 On this whole episode, see Stephen Jay Gould, 1999, *Rocks of Ages: Science and Religion in the Fullness of Life*, New York: Ballantine Books, pp. 111–24.

More recently, the allegation of an all-out, open warfare between science and Christianity – without denying the existence of, or damage done by, certain skirmishes of varying import – should be, at the very least, complicated by three further facts: Gregor Mendel, the nineteenth-century discoverer of genetics and thus the supplier of a vital missing piece in Darwin's theory, was an Augustinian monk; no less than 35 of the Moon's craters are named in honour of Jesuit scientists and mathematicians; and the Big Bang theory of the universe's beginning was first theorized by the Belgian priest (and eminent cosmologist) Georges Lemaître in 1931. Structured around these three claims, one might construct a history of how the Catholic Church has been the prime mover of modern scientific discovery. One would, however, be foolish to do so: *not* because any of these three statements is false (they're not), but because such cherry-picking cannot hope to represent a remotely accurate picture of so large, complex and contentious a topic as the one in question. The same is true for any parallel attempt to do the opposite on the basis of the Galileo affair, or a made-up retelling of Columbus at Salamanca.

Yet overblown, point-scoring claims, from *either* side, must not distract us from the crucial significance that modern scientific discoveries, especially some of those in the fields of physics and biology, hold for Christian theology. Famously, Sigmund Freud once cited Copernicus and Darwin as initiating the first two great, but humbling, revolutions in human thought – the first displacing the Earth as the centre of the universe, the second relegating humanity to just another animal species. While one may not agree with Freud's assessment, he is certainly correct in affirming the import of these discoveries. And it is largely upon these that the prevalent view that science has eroded the plausibility of Christianity (or 'religion' in general) is founded.

Of the two, it is the Darwinian revolution that is almost certainly the most troubling for Christianity. Modern astrophysics, ultimately flowing from the Copernican revolution, is actually a rather fertile ground for Christian metaphysical speculation and argumentation. For instance, the Big Bang cosmological model, which predicts a near-instantaneous 'beginning' of the universe at some definite point in the remote past, suffered in its early decades from the suspicion that it was simply a front for the Christian doctrine of 'creation out of nothing'.[13] Furthermore, the apparently 'finely tuned' nature of the universe (such that a minuscule difference in the 'strength' of one of several fundamental physical laws would have rendered the development of life – and indeed much of a universe at all – impossible) appears to some to betray the hand of a Creator with an interest in providing the necessary conditions for life to develop.

By contrast, Darwin's theory of natural selection, and the overwhelming observational confirmation it has received since first proposed over 150 years ago,[14] poses significant prima facie challenges to Christianity. Most obviously, it explains the manifold complexity and diversity in the biological world as the product of the gradual accumulation and refinement of inherited characteristics, in place of explaining each instance as a special creation of God. In itself, and contrary to popular belief, that is not so great

---

13 Simon Singh, *Big Bang: The Most Important Scientific Discovery of All Time and Why You Need to Know About It*, London: Fourth Estate, p. 361.

14 See, e.g., Richard Dawkins, 2009, *The Greatest Show on Earth: The Evidence for Evolution*, London: Bantam Press.

a problem for traditional Christian theology as one might assume: there is a long history in the Christian tradition of interpreting Genesis 1—3 as though it *isn't* intended as a scientific textbook (St Augustine's *Literal Interpretation of Genesis* being, contrary to the impression its title might give, a case in point), and even within a few years of *The Origin of Species*' original publication, so conservative a theologian as John Henry Newman expressed few qualms at the thought of 'going the whole hog with Darwin'.[15] What Darwin's theory did do, however, was overcome an obvious flaw in the pre-Darwinian naturalistic world view. Richard Dawkins puts it well, and is right to identify it as a watershed moment in the intuitive plausibility of unbelief:

An atheist before Darwin could have said, following Hume: 'I have no explanation for complex biological design. All I know is that God isn't a good explanation, so we must wait and hope that somebody comes up with a better one.' I can't help feeling that such a position, though logically sound, would have left one feeling pretty unsatisfied, and that although atheism might have been *logically* tenable before Darwin, Darwin made it possible to be an intellectually fulfilled atheist.[16]

Much more problematic for Christian theology, considered in itself, however, are the challenges that 'this view of life' (as Darwin referred to his theory) poses to a number of

15 Quoted in Don O'Leary, 2006, *Roman Catholicism and Modern Science*, New York: Continuum, p. 18.

16 Richard Dawkins, 1986, *The Blind Watchmaker: Why the Evidence of Evolution Reveals a Universe without Design*, New York: Norton, p. 6.

core Christian doctrines, not least the fall, original sin and providence. The American theologian John Haught is right to note that, in the wake of Darwin, Christian theologians have generally 'been slow to integrate into [their] theologies the four-billion-year evolutionary story of life's struggling, striving, and suffering'.[17] Neither Haught nor I believe that the challenges posed by Darwin are insuperable to orthodox Christian theology. Nevertheless, he cites the fact that many theologians, while formally accepting Darwinism, continue nonchalantly to write and think about humanity, sin and salvation without feeling the need to grapple with these issues explicitly. This, Haught suggests, gives the *impression* that there is, after all, an impassable gulf between modern scientific knowledge and the Christian faith, such that: 'For many educated people, therefore, embracing [Christian] faith still seems to require an ignoring, if not suppression, of some of the most important truths they have learned from the natural sciences.'[18] And if this is true of people who do, nevertheless, see enough of what is true in Christianity to want to subscribe to it, how much more must it reinforce the impressions of others that even if there is not, after all, a necessary conflict between 'science' and 'religion', there nevertheless is between Darwin and orthodox Christianity. As the intellectual 'reasons to disbelieve' go, then, this is surely one that requires a great deal more thought on the part of believers.

---

17 John F. Haught, 2009, 'Darwin, Divine Providence, and the Suffering of Sentient Life', in Louis Caruana (ed.), *Darwin and Catholicism: The Past and Present Dynamics of a Cultural Encounter*, London: T & T Clark, pp. 207–22, at p. 207.

18 Haught, *Darwin and Catholicism*, p. 208.

Conclusion

In this chapter we have covered a great deal of ground, and covered it rather swiftly. The intellectual reasons for atheism (and, relatedly though not identically, the intellectual reasons against Christianity) constitute a vast and varied field. As such, all that has really been possible here has been some brief reflections on what are arguably the three most significant: the radical nature of the Christian message itself; the nature and extent of suffering in the world; and the perceived disjunction between faith and scientific discovery (a perception arguably not helped by believers themselves). In all three cases far more could, and perhaps should, have been written.

That said, however, despite the undoubted importance of these – and other – intellectual factors, as argued earlier, it is a mistake to reduce the *reasons* for unbelief to these alone. Intellectual arguments and ideas are only ever apprehended and entertained within complex contexts made up of a wide range of overlapping and interlocking factors: historical, social, psychological, historical, economic and political. This is, of course, why certain ideas that *seem* so plain and obvious to us here and now, might seem odd or even abhorrent in other times or places – and vice versa. Likewise, on a personal level the exact same argument that has left us cold at one stage in our lives might seem vital and compelling at a later one. It is not the argument that has changed but rather one or both of the backgrounds against which we consider it, and who we are who are doing the receiving. On that note, it is time to look at the background against and the context within which the Christian faith is being proposed – and to consider why, for many people, it seems to be rather less plausible than it was in the past.

3

'Is it not our own fault?'

The title of this chapter is a quotation from the Catholic theologian Henri de Lubac, commenting on the growth of ill-informed, atheistic critiques of Christianity in 1930s France.[1] Without denying the *possibility* of wilful ignorance, scholarly laziness or sheer intellectual dishonesty on the part of its sharpest critics, if caricatures of Christianity are prevalent and plausible-seeming, then it seems likely that Christians have failed somewhat in explaining and communicating the authentic version. De Lubac's question recognizes that if otherwise intelligent and knowledgeable thinkers are advancing theologically illiterate objections to the Christian faith, and if these criticisms appear justified and plausible to significant numbers of people, then Christians themselves must take some responsibility.

The basic point here does not just apply to intellectual reasons for unbelief. As briefly pointed out in this book's Introduction, atheism is predominantly a feature of historically Christian countries, and many of the world's most unbelieving populations may be found in Europe, in the heart of what used to be (and still is, though less convincingly)

---

1 Henri de Lubac, [1938] 1964, *Catholicism: A Study of Dogma in Relation to the Corporate Destiny of Mankind*, trans. Lancelot C. Sheppard, New York: Mentor-Omega, p. xi.

called *Christendom*. Significant too is the fact that western atheism, both positive and negative, is an overwhelmingly native, indigenous, home-grown phenomenon. The growth and spread of unbelief over the past three hundred years, slowly at first but rapidly accelerating in the past century or so, has not been the result of some potent influx of ideas from outside. It arose out of the intellectual, social, cultural and political world of Europe, a world that had been shaped and dominated by Christianity for well over a millennium.

In itself, unbelief is neither an original nor unique creation of modern Europe. It was not entirely unheard of in ancient Greece and Rome, and Psalms 14 and 53 possibly testify to its existence among the ancient Hebrews. There were also well-established atheistic (if not necessarily 'non-supernaturalistic') schools and movements in ancient India as far back as the middle of the first millennium BC.[2] Yet it was not time-travelling missionaries from ancient Greece, Rome or India who introduced atheism to Europe in the early eighteenth century. One of modern Europe's first, identifiable atheists was a French Catholic priest by the name of Jean Meslier.[3]

Though Meslier kept quiet while alive, upon his death in 1729 was found a *Testament* addressed to his parishioners, denouncing organized religion in general and dismissing the Gods of both Christianity and deism. Importantly Meslier's arguments against Christianity, and theism in general, are not drawn from earlier atheistic sources. Nor does he devise

---

2 See Jessica Frazier, 2013, 'Hinduism', in Stephen Bullivant and Michael Ruse (eds), *The Oxford Handbook of Atheism*, Oxford: Oxford University Press.

3 See Michel Onfray, 2007, *Atheist Manifesto: The Case Against Christianity, Judaism, and Islam*, trans. Jeremy Leggatt, New York: Arcade Publishing, pp. 28–9.

original ones for himself. Instead, the bulk of his criticisms are adapted from the writings of contemporary *theologians*. He especially drew on the acrimonious, mutual refutations of each other's ideas by the rival French theological schools, with each attempting to demonstrate how the others' ideas were, at root, tantamount to atheism. Thus, as Alan Charles Kors has written recently: 'With relentlessness and skill, the dialecticians of early-modern learned France taught readers to find the atheistic naturalism of all systems.'[4]

The general notion that key strands of early-modern atheistic thought ultimately have specifically theological roots is an important, if contested, notion in much recent scholarship on the topic. As Alister McGrath has pithily put it: 'nobody really doubted the existence of God until theologians tried to prove it'.[5] The basic idea here is, however, not wholly new. Writing some decades before the recent crop of historical studies, the Swiss theologian Hans Urs von Balthasar argued: 'It is more difficult for modern man than it was for previous generations to see the world as an epiphany, as a revelation of, and a reference to, God . . . and Christianity played a part in this change.'[6]

The above considerations, while no doubt instructive, ought not to be overstated. Quite how atheism was begotten in early-modern Europe, and the extent to which it was or wasn't born from explicitly Christian sources, is largely an academic question. Whosoever its parents (or ancestors)

---

4 Alan Charles Kors, 2013, 'The Age of Enlightenment', in Stephen Bullivant and Michael Ruse (eds), *The Oxford Handbook of Atheism*, Oxford: Oxford University Press.

5 Alister McGrath, 2004, *The Twilight of Atheism: The Rise and Fall of Disbelief in the Modern World*, London: Rider, p. 31.

6 Hans Urs von Balthasar, 1965, 'Meeting God in Today's World', trans. James F. McCue, *Concilium* 6/1, pp. 14–22, at p. 14.

may have been, there is no doubting that, three hundred years on, western unbelief has most assuredly gained its independence, come of age and left the family home. Undue focus on abstract philosophical and theological discussions, in and around the Enlightenment, also obscures the fact that strictly intellectual factors are far from the only significant ones when it comes to faith and unbelief. It would be fair to say that the huge growth of popular unbelief in the west, which began in earnest – at least in much of western Europe and (later, and more slowly) in Canada, Australia and now the United States – probably as late as the 1960s, is not *primarily* due to the spread of the ideas of Jean Meslier or Voltaire, or even of Bertrand Russell, Madalyn Murray O'Hair or Richard Dawkins. Instead, one needs to look at a complex of overlapping social, cultural and economic factors, not all of them very obvious. To give just one example: the relativizing effects of the growth of travel and the media in the twentieth century, in tandem with rising multiculturalism and religious plurality, may also have had a major, if subtle, influence on the erstwhile taken-for-granted nature of one's own religious position – and, by extension, of needing to have a religious position at all.

Against so rich and multifaceted a backdrop, which we are very far from having done justice to in these brief remarks,[7] it would be arrogant of Christians to assume full credit (or blame) for either the intellectual or socio-cultural causes of atheism in our time. The birth, growth, vitality and – to a large and increasing number of people – plausibility of positive or negative atheism cannot simply be ascribed to the

---

7 See the 'Further reading' section for some interesting and in many ways contrasting perspectives on secularization (and, relatedly though not synonymously, 'atheization').

negligence or absentmindedness of Christians. Nevertheless, it is surely true that an honest answer to de Lubac's question must yield at least a partial 'yes'. At the simplest and thus probably most important level, confirmation of this can be found by reading the 'deconversion' accounts of those who have become atheists, which often cite some specific criticism, real or perceived, justified or not, of Christian thought and/ or practice as a key reason or catalyst, even if it is not the only one.[8] Recognizing this basic fact, and without denying the existence and importance of other factors too, the Second Vatican Council's 1965 statement on modern atheism – which, not incidentally, de Lubac helped to draft – admitted that:

> [B]elievers can have no small part in the rise of atheism, since by neglecting education in the faith, teaching false doctrine, or through defects in their own religious, moral or social lives, they may be said rather more to conceal than reveal the true countenance of God and of religion. (*Gaudium et Spes*, 19)

In the rest of this chapter I would like to explore some of these ideas – the intellectual, moral, social and religious ways in which Christians 'may be said rather more to conceal than reveal' the Most True God. There are, to be sure, lots of these. Here, though, we will focus on just three: what Thomas Aquinas called the *irrisio infidelium* ('the mockery of unbelievers'); the moral failings of Christians, individually and collectively; and the deep and lasting wounds of Christian disunity.

---

8 See, e.g., the testimonies collected in Phil Zuckerman, 2011, *Faith No More: Why People Reject Religion*, New York: Oxford University Press.

Irrisio infidelium

In a remarkable passage in St Augustine's notably un-literal *Literal Interpretation of Genesis*, he urges his fellow believers against making rash, 'Bible-based' pronouncements on scientific topics. Augustine points out that a great many non-Christians are well informed on subjects such as astronomy, zoology, botany and geology, and that they regard their knowledge of these matters 'to be certain from reason and experience'. As such:

> [I]t is a disgraceful and dangerous thing for an unbeliever to hear a Christian, presumably giving the meaning of Holy Scripture, talking nonsense on these topics; and we should take all means to prevent such an embarrassing situation, in which people show up a Christian's vast ignorance and laugh it to scorn. (*Literal Interpretation*, I, xix, 39)[9]

Augustine's point is that such non-Christians, on hearing such misguided views attributed to the Scriptures, will come to dismiss and deride Christianity itself. He adds pointedly:

> If they find a Christian mistaken in a field which they themselves know well and hear him maintaining his foolish opinions about our books, how are they going to believe those books in matters concerning the resurrection of the dead, the hope of eternal life, and the kingdom of heaven, when they think their pages are full of falsehoods on facts which they themselves have learnt from experience and the light of reason?

---

9 Translation from John H. Taylor (ed.), 1982, *Augustine, Vol. I: The Literal Meaning of Genesis*, Mahwah, NJ: Paulist Press, pp. 42–3.

Augustine proceeds to lambaste these 'reckless and incompetent expounders of Holy Scripture' who, in order 'to defend their utterly foolish and obviously untrue statements', cite memorized biblical proof–texts 'which they think support their position', despite the fact that (quoting 1 Tim. 1.7) 'they don't understand either what they are saying or the things about which they are making assertions'.

Several centuries later, writing in the second book of his commentary on Peter Lombard's *Sentences*, Thomas Aquinas heeds Augustine's warning. Adjudicating between differing interpretations of Genesis 1, each championed by learned and saintly commentators, Thomas errs *against* the commoner and seemingly more literal one, primarily on the grounds that the other better protects Scripture from 'the mockery of unbelievers' (*irrisio infidelium*).[10] Thomas' reasoning here might strike us as strange,[11] at least if it is understood as a purely 'apologetic' decision; that is, as springing from a desire to present Christian doctrine in the most enticing possible light, in order to lure

---

10 *Sentences*, 2.2, d. 12, a. 2. Quotations from this text will be taken from Ralph McInerny (ed.), 1998, *Thomas Aquinas: Selected Writings*, London: Penguin, pp. 91–2. McInerny, however, translates *irrisio infidelium* as 'the derision of infidels', whereas 'mockery of unbelievers' is preferred here.

11 The precise point at issue relates to the question of whether, in the beginning, God created all things simultaneously, or in a number of successive stages (as Genesis, with its 'day-by-day' narration, seems to imply). Perhaps surprisingly, it is the former position that Thomas admits is 'more pleasing to me' for the reasons already given. However – heeding also Augustine's cautions against siding too strongly with a single interpretation of a scriptural text that can legitimately support several, lest 'if further progress in the search of truth justly undermines this position, we too fall with it' – Thomas lays aside his own stated preference in order to present the arguments for both sides.

in unsuspecting outsiders. This is not, however, Thomas's point at all. Instead, like Augustine, he acknowledges the wisdom and knowledge that many unbelievers have on certain scientific and philosophical matters. Hence, provided that no essential point of the Christian Faith is at issue (a point to which we shall return), if a particular *interpretation* of Scripture is likely to give rise to such mockery, then that is, in itself, a decent indication that it might well not be the correct one.

Augustine and Thomas raise an important point, and one that applies far more widely than the correct interpretation of Genesis (though this, of course, remains an important area – probably more so now than it was in their times). It is a very commonly heard complaint that such-and-such an atheist writer is merely dismantling straw men, critiquing 'old man in the sky' caricatures, tilting at theological windmills; that the God whom Friedrich Nietzsche or Bertrand Russell or Madalyn Murray O'Hair or Sam Harris *doesn't* believe in, isn't the same one that Christians *do*. Many of these criticisms are, no doubt, true enough (though as pointed out in Chapter 1, it doesn't follow that all such criticisms always must be!). But we come back, once again, to the question of *who* precisely is to blame for this. If Christian theology is so susceptible to cartoon-ish misrepresentations, and if Christians themselves have gained a reputation, however false, for being irrational, childishly wishful thinkers, then this has certainly not arisen out of nothing. At least some of the windmills tilted at, perhaps, are ones that believers themselves have had a hand in constructing. After all, it doesn't take a herculean effort of intellectual empathy to see why an unbeliever *might* (wrongly) think that Christians extol 'faith' as being 'blind trust, in the absence of evidence, even in the teeth of evidence'[12] or *might* (wrongly) view the doctrine of the atonement as 'vicious, sado-masochistic and . . . barking mad'[13] or *might* (wrongly) regard St Anselm's ontological argument to be 'infantile' and best suited 'to the language of the playground'.[14] Note that these are all quotations from a person brought up in a Christian country, who was baptized and who spent his formative years at a Christian school.

Recall Vatican II's identification of Christians' 'neglecting education in the faith' and 'teaching false doctrine' as factors in the prevalence of atheism. Either one might easily lead to engendering the justified mockery of unbelievers – mockery that, as Augustine stresses, is mistakenly directed at Christianity itself. Yet Augustine is, perhaps, overly harsh to his 'reckless and incompetent expounders of Holy Scripture'. For it is indeed a difficult and daunting task to understand, expound and explain authentic Christian teaching on the vast range of topics that people might ask about and in a manner that does justice to what one is hoping faithfully to represent. Fear of exciting the *irrisio infidelium* must, moreover, surely be tempered by fidelity to the injunction in 1 Peter 3.15: 'Always be ready to make your defence to anyone who demands from you an account of the hope that is in you; yet do it with gentleness and reverence.' The middle ground here, presumably, is for believers to make a real effort to learn more about the faith that they profess, to seek out trustworthy teachers and writers and to strive to understand better why it is that

---

12 Richard Dawkins, [1976] 1989, *The Selfish Gene*, 2nd edn, Oxford: Oxford University Press, p. 198.

13 Richard Dawkins, 2006, *The God Delusion*, London: Bantam Press, p. 253.

14 Dawkins, *God Delusion*, p. 80.

Christianity affirms certain things – *especially* those that might at first sight seem to be obviously false, obviously repellent or obviously both. And furthermore, that they do so not only for their own sakes but for the sakes of (in Augustine's phrase) 'people outside the household of the faith . . . for whose salvation we toil' (*Literal Interpretation*, I, xix, 39). Indeed, to paraphrase Henri de Lubac: if so many people are so grievously mistaken about the essence of Christianity, is it not an indication that Christians should make an effort to understand it better themselves?[15]

The issue of *irrisio infidelium* raises another equally important point. The last chapter noted just how important it is for theologians properly to think through Christian doctrine in light of new scientific discoveries, the Darwinian revolution and its myriad implications chief among them. And indeed, the above–quoted passages from Augustine could just as easily have been written, word for word, in the present day: those even passingly acquainted with modern biology can, and do, find much to mock in many Christians' assertions regarding the meaning of Genesis 1. In contexts such as these, our two great saints do well to counsel contemporary believers against needlessly scandalizing outsiders and thus prejudicing them against Christianity.

Avoiding the 'mockery of unbelievers' is *not*, however, an absolute, overriding norm for theology. Thomas, in particular, is careful to distinguish between things pertaining to 'the substance of the faith' ('such that God is three and one, and the like'), and other less essential beliefs, upon which a greater latitude of opinion is possible. For Thomas, the affirmation that the world was created by God belongs to the former

---

15 De Lubac's original formulation refers explicitly to 'Catholicism' rather than to Christianity in general (Lubac, p. xi).

category, whereas certain, technical points about quite *how* it was brought about – 'matters [on which] even the saints disagree, explaining scripture in different ways'[16] – belong to the latter. For Thomas, if the very notion that 'God created the heavens and the earth' (Gen. 1.1) spurs unbelievers' derision, then so much the worse for the unbelievers. But learned and well-informed unbelievers might well have valid opinions about some of the 'details' of quite how it was brought about, and one must be careful not to scandalize them needlessly. (He goes so far as to write that, in these cases, 'Scripture must be explained in such a way that the unbeliever cannot mock'.) Importantly, though, what neither Thomas nor Augustine is here prescribing is a kind of carte blanche to modify or dilute the 'substance of faith' to suit the whims of the day. Atheists' incredulity towards, say, the incarnation, resurrection or even the existence of God is not a legitimate ground for reinterpreting Christianity in any 'demythologized' way. As argued in the previous chapter, authentic Christianity is committed to certain claims that are and ought to be, at least at first sight, 'foolishness to Gentiles' (1 Cor. 1.23). The intellectual bowdlerization of the gospel, and all other such (undoubtedly well-meaning) attempts to domesticate the Christian message, are just as much cases of 'teaching false doctrine' as is, say, insisting that Christianity is necessarily committed to Young Earth Creationism (which, if it was, would make heretics of Augustine and Thomas). To be sure, it may well be difficult to discern what is and is not essential to the 'substance of faith'; the dividing line between 'foolishness to Gentiles', and 'mockery of unbelievers', might well be a fine one. Even so, it is well to remember that there is more than one way 'rather more to conceal than reveal' the Most True God.

---

16 McInerny (ed.), *Thomas Aquinas: Selected Writings*, p. 91.

A school for scandal?

Joachim Kahl, a former Lutheran pastor whose incisive 1971 book, *The Misery of Christianity,* prefigures much in more recent atheist works, once commented: 'the history of Christianity is the best school for atheism'.[17] It is not hard to see what he is getting at. Christianity's path through the past two millennia is littered with scandals, and has been from the beginning. One of Jesus' own closest friends and confidants, the man entrusted with the disciples' finances, was prepared to betray him for a modest sum of money. (Later portrayals – such as in Andrew Lloyd Webber's musical *Jesus Christ Superstar* – like to depict Judas' actions as stemming from disillusioned idealism, but the actual sources themselves suggest no higher motive than cash in hand.) The rest of the New Testament records for us a catalogue of failings by some of the earliest Christians, including, but by no means limited to: financial fraud (Acts 5.1–11); sexual impropriety, drunkenness, robbery, litigiousness, greed and avarice (1 Cor. 5.1 – 6.8, 11.17–22; Gal. 5.19–21); 'obscene, silly, and vulgar talk' (Eph. 5.4; see also James 3); and toadying up to the rich while neglecting the poor (James 2).

Later history demonstrates, moreover, that these were not just teething problems for the Christian community, merely initial difficulties in stripping 'off the old self' (Col. 3.9). In teaching a whistle-stop overview of Church history to my first-year undergraduates, two episodes in particular are guaranteed a horrified reception: Pope Stephen VI's exhumation of Pope Formosus' corpse, to have him tried and posthumously deposed at the aptly named 'cadaver

17 Joachim Kahl, 1971, *The Misery of Christianity: A Plea for Humanity without God,* trans. N. D. Smith, London: Pelican, p. 15.

synod' of 897; and the Fourth Crusade of 1202–4, in which the Catholic crusaders first ravaged the also-Catholic city of Zara on the coast of Croatia, then besieged and sacked the Orthodox centre of Constantinople. In our own time, Christians of one sort or another have, individually and collectively, been responsible for all manner of atrocities. To name only some of the more heinous: the war crimes of Joseph Kony's 'Lord's Resistance Army' in Uganda; Anders Breivik's massacre of Norwegian youths and politicians in 2011; and the sexual abuse of minors and subsequent cover-ups in Europe, America and elsewhere.[18]

Of course, it is easily possible to overstate the case on this point. For example, it is not that uncommon to meet with the view, stated as though it were an uncontroversial and obvious matter of fact, that Christianity (along with 'religion-in-general') has had a near-catastrophic effect on pretty well every aspect of human moral and social life. Conversely, it is often implied that if all religions were swept away, then the whole of humanity would be vastly happier and better off. Often this kind of view is accompanied by the assertion that whatever good *can* be found in either Christian moral teaching, or in the conduct of individual Christians, is platitudinous or plagiarized.

What one *might* do at this juncture is point out the radical and distinctive nature of Christian moral teaching and

---

18 Of course, there is a question here regarding the extent to which the perpetrators of such crimes can genuinely be considered 'Christians'. That said, it is all too easy to avoid the issue at hand by discounting 'bad' Christians as not being Christians at all. In any case, for our purposes here the fact that such people call themselves Christians is itself sufficient cause for scandal (in roughly the same way as, for Augustine, those claiming their own erroneous views on science to be Christian ones, even if false, engender scandal enough in the eyes of unbelievers).

practice, and the revolution its advent wrought on western culture and society. Without failing to admit and lament the repeated and sometimes catastrophic moral failings of Christians, one could cite the ethical and social sea change gradually brought about by a small group of first-century provincials' conviction that the Lord of the Universe had ordered (in the words of the first-century *Didache*, a 'manual' for new Christian communities written during the New Testament period):

> Commit no murder, adultery, sodomy, fornication, or theft. Practise no magic, sorcery, abortion, or infanticide. See that you do not covet anything your neighbour possesses, and never be guilty of perjury, false witness, slander, or malice. Do not equivocate in thought or speech, for a double tongue is a deadly snare; the words you speak should not be false or empty phrase . . . You are not to be avaricious or extortionate, and you must resist any temptation to hypocrisy, spitefulness, or superiority. You are to have no malicious designs on a neighbour. You are to cherish no feelings of hatred for anybody; some you are to reprove, some to pray for, and some again to love more than your own life. (*Didache*, 2)[19]

The originality of the above, the challenge it posed to the surrounding culture and its ongoing – if, disturbingly, now perhaps fading – legacy down to the present day are important, apologetic points of response to the kinds of criticism sketched above.

---

19 Translation from Maxwell Staniforth (trans.), 1968, *Early Christian Writings*, Harmondsworth: Penguin, p. 228.

However, the real point at issue here is somewhat more complicated. Simply making the (valid and necessary) case that *overall* Christianity has been, and still is, a force for good – that the positives outweigh the negatives, or the Mother Teresas trump the Fourth Crusaders, yielding a kind of 'net gain' for humanity – rather misses the mark regarding Christian history being 'the best school for atheism'. Indeed, the very fact that we are reduced to talking in such terms is revealing. In Chapter 2 we discussed the radical nature of the Christian proclamation. Measured against the preaching of its founder, actual Christian practice doesn't always bear up so well. The Sermon on the Mount is not obviously an injunction for Christians to be, all things considered, *something* of an improvement. One is reminded of G. K. Chesterton's famous remark: 'The Christian ideal has not been tried and found wanting. It has been found difficult; and left untried.'[20]

According to Scripture, Christians have, through baptism, 'died to sin' (Rom. 6.2) and 'clothed' themselves in Christ (Gal. 3.27). Furthermore, they are 'children of God', 'heirs of God and joint heirs with Christ' (Rom. 8.17), and 'as God's chosen ones, holy and beloved' ought therefore to 'clothe [themselves] with compassion, kindness, humility, meekness, and patience' (Col. 3.12). Such statements ought not, of course, to be understood naively. Nevertheless, there is no denying that these are exalted, grandiose claims to be making of anyone, and especially of oneself (in so far as one claims to be a Christian). Against such claims, it is no wonder that Christian failings provide so much 'ammunition'. The scandal here is not so much that Christians, being

---

20 Philip Schall (ed.), [1910] 1987, *The Collected Works of G. K. Chesterton*, Vol. 4, San Francisco, CA: Ignatius Press, p. 4.

human beings, have the capacity to commit sin. Rather, the scandal is that they do so, and so lavishly, against so extravagant a backdrop of moral teaching and example. The ultimate reasons for this contradiction between theory and practice lie, of course, in human freedom and original sin. (Chesterton, with his typical sharp-eyed irreverence, once also remarked that original sin 'is the only part of Christian doctrine which can really be proved'.)[21] But that hardly makes it – or, to the outsider's eyes, makes it appear – any the less hypocritical.

Note well that it is *hypocrisy* specifically, not just immorality itself, that is a charge so often directed at Christians, and one frequently cited as a specific factor in motivating an individual's unbelief.[22] Failing to 'walk the walk' is bad enough; failing to walk it while ostentatiously 'talking the talk' is all the more unforgivable. In fact, recent research in the field of cognitive anthropology suggests that human beings have specifically evolved to trust beliefs and ideas whose proposers actually live out the costly implications of them and conversely, to be mistrustful of those whose proposers do not.[23] As such, we are probably more likely to find an argument for the truth of Christianity convincing if it is put forward by someone who actually does 'take up their cross and follow me' (hence the reason why 'the blood of the martyrs is the seed of the church', as Tertullian famously

21 G. K. Chesterton, [1908] 1996, *Orthodoxy*, ed. Philip Yancey, London: Hodder & Stoughton, p. 10.

22 It is also, perhaps, why so much more attention – and anger – seems to be directed towards cases of sexual abuse within church communities, as opposed to similar cases in secular contexts such as schools or social services.

23 See, e.g., Jonathan A. Lanman, 2012, 'The Importance of Religious Displays for Belief Acquisition and Secularization', *Journal of Contemporary Religion* 27/1, pp. 49–65.

put it). By contrast, invitations to become disciples of Jesus Christ are not only unconvincing, but are indeed actively repellent, on the lips of those who 'are corrupt, [and] commit abominable acts' (Ps 14.1, 53.1). This is a point to which we shall return in Chapter 6.

Denomination blues

The Texas gospel singer Washington Phillips (1880–1954) used to sing a song called 'Denomination Blues'. This largely consists of a rundown of the idiosyncratic customs of different Christian groups. He notes, for example: 'The Primitive Baptists, they believe, you can't get to heaven unless they wash your feet.' The Missionary Baptists, meanwhile, insist that the essential thing is 'to go under the water and not to wash the feet'. This is in stark contrast to the Indian Methodists, however, who find it necessary 'to sprinkle the head and not to wash the feet', and so on. Commenting on these differences, and the disagreements to which they give rise, Phillips sings:

> You're fighting each other, and think you're doing well;
> and the sinner's on the outside, going to hell.
> And that's all now, I tell you that's all.
> But you better have Jesus now, I tell you that's all.

While we will offer reasons in the next chapter for a slightly more hopeful outlook on the outsider's post–mortem fate, Phillips' basic point is an important one. Effectively, he is arguing that divisions among Christians themselves are a major cause of evangelistic failure, and are a significant reason why outsiders (whether atheists or not) remain so.

Roughly the same idea occurs in the Gospel of John, where Jesus prays to his Father on behalf of the disciples: 'Holy Father, protect them in your name that you have given me, so that they may be one, as we are one' (John 17.11). This petition, that his followers might both reflect and participate in the unity that the Father and the Son themselves enjoy, is justified in terms of the nascent Church's mission to those outside:

> I ask not only on behalf of these, but also on behalf of those who will believe in me through their word, that they may all be one. As you, Father, are in me and I am in you, may they also be in us, so that the world may believe that you have sent me. The glory that you have given me I have given them, so that they may be one, as we are one, I in them and you in me, that they may become completely one, so that the world may know that you have sent me and have loved them even as you have loved me. (17.20–23)

It is perhaps a strange kind of comfort to Christians that even the prayers of Jesus himself sometimes go unanswered.

Christian dissension and discord is not, of course, a wholly modern phenomenon. From the earliest times, Church unity has been a fragile thing. That is why the early Fathers were so insistent on it, in the face of the constant threat of schism: groups of – to their eyes – breakaway (mis)believers, leading others astray and severing the bonds of communion. While most of these were relatively short lived, more significant and long-lasting divisions were not unknown, and at least two of note (following the Councils of Ephesus in 431 and the Council of Chalcedon in 451) have endured to the present day. The complex and gradual estrangement between East and West, leading eventually to the 'Great Schism' between the Catholic and Eastern Orthodox Churches, can also trace many of its roots to the patristic period. However, by the time that the Fourth Crusade's sack of Constantinople added the final *coup-de-grâce* to the faint hopes for Catholic–Orthodox unity in 1204, Christian divisiveness had barely got going. On the eve of the Reformation in the early sixteenth century, there was no more than a handful of distinct Christian Churches. Across the world today, by contrast, there are thousands of separate denominations.[24]

The part that denominational diversity may play in creating and sustaining contemporary atheism is, admittedly, a difficult one to pick apart. *Pace* Washington Phillips (and Jesus), one could argue that such plurality is, on balance, a good thing. If a person becomes disillusioned with one 'brand' of Christianity, then rather than have to abandon Christianity – and perhaps with it, ultimately, belief in God altogether – one can instead find another kind,

---

24 Understandably, it is difficult to give a more accurate figure than this. One often sees a figure of 38,000 quoted, drawn from the 2001 *World Christian Encyclopedia*. This, however, defines denomination as being a distinct Christian Church *within* a particular country. This yields some odd and counter–intuitive results, not least that the 'the Roman Catholic Church, although a single organization, is described here as consisting of 236 denominations in the world's 238 countries' (David Barrett et al. [eds], 2001, *World Christian Encyclopedia*, Vol. 1, 2nd edn, Oxford: Oxford University Press, p. 27). The same applies, of course, to many other cross-national denominations, leading to 38,000 representing a vastly and misleadingly inflated figure for most purposes. Other problems, however, arise from the diverse understandings of 'denomination' present within different Christian groups. Is, for example, each 'non-denominational' or 'independent' or 'simply Christian' church, which are so prominent in the USA, to be counted as a (mostly, though not always, very small) denomination in its own right? If so, then a 2010 census carried out by the Hartford Institute for Religion Research uncovered over 35,000 of them.

more suited to one's tastes. Thus the Primitive Baptist who renounces feet-washing, has the option of becoming a full-immersion Missionary Baptist, or else a head-sprinkling Indian Methodist, instead. Such an approach, albeit more subtly and rigorously fleshed out, is sometimes referred to as a 'marketplace model'. It has been argued, for example, that this is a key factor in explaining the notable buoyancy of American Christianity, and relative leadenness of American unbelief, when compared to the situation in western Europe. On this view, the sheer, competitive diversity of Christian offerings (in terms of theology, worship style, ethnic makeup) available in the USA is contrasted favourably with the European model of quasi-monopolistic Established Churches. Quoting Robert Putnam, for example: 'religion in America (unlike in most other advanced Western nations) has been pluralistic and constantly evolving, expressed in a kaleidoscopic series of revivals and awakenings rather than a single-state religion that could become ossified.'[25]

Whatever the merits or not of this sociological argument, it is certainly true that a rather different case can be made concerning Christian disunity's role in the rise and prevalence of atheism. Earlier in this chapter it was noted how bitter, internecine theological disputes in seventeenth-century France aided the developing scepticism towards *all* theological arguments exhibited by Meslier, Voltaire and others. The divided – or rather, since the Reformation, *splintered* or *shattered* – state of Christianity arguably replicates this, albeit on a far vaster canvas. Quite apart from the tragic record of

---

25 Robert D. Putnam, 2000, *Bowling Alone: The Collapse and Revival of American Community*, New York: Simon & Schuster, p. 66.

violence between Christians of different types (which is itself frequently cited by unbelievers as proof of the pernicious effects of Christian and indeed all religious belief), the many theological disagreements between denominations can easily give the impression, however false, that Christians are not actually disagreeing about anything *real* at all.

Not that, in itself, there is anything wrong about disagreement and debate about matters of genuine substance: indeed, on such matters frank but respectful disagreement is almost always to be preferred to false irenicism and the pretence of harmony. Yet that is not always how it looks to an outsider. Consider, for example, how common it is for people, on seeing two economists disagree on the best policy to get out of recession, to dismiss the entire validity of economics as a subject ('The economists can't even agree among themselves!'), or on hearing two conflicting weather reports, to express scepticism about meteorology itself ('Oh, they're just making it up!'). Now consider how it must seem to an unbeliever (or a wavering believer) when they notice that on almost all the supposedly key doctrines of Christianity – creation, the Virgin birth, the incarnation, the resurrection, the Eucharist, eschatology – there are not only huge and sometimes vociferous disagreements between individuals, but that many of the different views on these topics can often be found enshrined as a certain, non-negotiably necessary article of faith in one or other of the denominations. Given that even on such core principles the denominations not only do not agree but affirm mutually exclusive positions, it is no surprise if people are led to assume that they are not, after all, disagreeing about matters of actual fact. Even though they *are* – just like economists and meteorologists are! – one can perhaps see why David Hume's remark that 'in matters of religion, whatever is different is contrary'[26] might come readily to mind.

The above is not, it should be noted, a call for the Christian communities to jettison dogmatic differences (and with them, inevitably, dogma itself), to pretend that they do not exist or to kid themselves that they do not matter.[27] A move towards an enervated, 'doctrine-lite' form of Christianity is scarcely a response to the problems posed by unbelief – indeed, as I have argued in Chapter 2, it is precisely the distinctive, 'hard' teachings of traditional Christianity that need to be emphasized and explained anew. (It is perhaps worth noting here that the Christian groups in Europe and America that are gaining more people than they are losing – notably pentecostal and evangelical ones – can hardly be accused of pulling their doctrinal punches.) Yet that need not prevent us from echoing, with considerable sorrow, the French Dominican Yves Congar's words: 'Concretely, the division among Christians is a scandal for the world. The world is exonerated, to a degree, from the duty to believe.'[28]

_____

26 David Hume, [1748] 2007, *An Inquiry Concerning Human Understanding and Other Essays*, ed. Stephen Buckle, Cambridge: Cambridge University Press, p. 106.

27 Incidentally, I once visited the campus of Liverpool Hope University, which was set up as an explicitly ecumenical, joint Anglican–Catholic foundation. Accordingly the chapel has two tabernacles – one Anglican, one Catholic – side by side. In one sense, this is a painful, visible expression of Christian disunity. Given the sad fact of this disunity, however, this kind of 'Chalcedonian' settlement ('fully Anglican and fully Catholic') struck me as being far preferable to the 'neater' alternative of having no tabernacle at all ('neither Anglican nor Catholic'). I was also prompted to think how many times this jarring juxtaposition must have prompted visitors to the chapel to make Jesus' prayer, 'that they may be one', their own.

28 Yves Congar, 1962, 'The Council in an Age of Dialogue', trans. Barry N. Rigney, *Cross Currents* 12, pp. 144–51, at p. 148.

Conclusion

Even more so than the others, this chapter has adopted something of a scattergun approach. It has treated a number of what are, in themselves, wholly separate and self-contained subjects – the intellectual roots of modern western atheism; Augustine and Aquinas on interpreting Scripture; the tawdry and shadowy aspects of Christian malpractice; ecclesial discord and disharmony – and has simply placed them side by side, juxtaposed, with little by the way of unifying threads between them. The result may, perhaps, seem like something akin to a shipwreck, a jarring and confusing mess of things, out of which it is hard to make any kind of simplistic sense. If so, I dare say that there's a metaphor in there somewhere.

In this chapter and the previous one, we have been trying to understand the reasons behind the meteoric growth of various types of atheism over the past few centuries (most of all in the past fifty or so years), and particularly its current prevalence and vitality. It is worth stating, once again, how great a novelty this phenomenon is, and how outlandish it would have seemed to the vast majority of the thinkers and writers – the Psalmist, the New Testament authors, Augustine, Thomas Aquinas – who nevertheless are helping us to make some kind of Christian sense of it. It should come as no surprise, then, that the 'reasons to disbelieve' are many and complex. Even among the selected few we have focused on here, we have witnessed a heady mix of social, cultural, philosophical, scientific, moral, historical and theological factors at work.

Christians themselves, individually and collectively, undoubtedly have played – and still do play – their part in all of this. Indeed each of us, knowingly or not, and in countless ways big and small, have done things that 'may be said rather more to conceal than reveal the true countenance of God' (*Gaudium et Spes*, 19). In itself, that is a fact worth reflecting upon, especially if – to quote yet another line from *The Brothers Karamazov* – 'each of us is guilty before everyone, for everyone and everything'.[29] Needless to say, it also has profound implications for what are, almost certainly, the cardinal themes in the whole ambit of 'faith and unbelief': salvation and evangelization. It is the first of these topics to which we now turn.

29 Fyodor Dostoevsky, [1880] 2004, *The Brothers Karamazov*, trans. Richard Pevear and Larissa Volokhonsky, London: Vintage, p.289.

4

Can atheists be saved?

In the Gospel of John, Jesus declares: 'I am the way, and the truth, and the life. No one comes to the Father except through me' (14.6). Earlier, he informs Nicodemus that 'no one can enter the kingdom of God without being born of water and Spirit' (3.5). In the epilogue to Mark's Gospel, Jesus is reported as telling the disciples: 'The one who believes and is baptized will be saved; but the one who does not believe will be condemned' (16.16). On the face of it, these are not promising statements concerning the salvation of *any* non-Christian, let alone the many millions of human beings – past, present and future – without even a belief in the existence of a God or gods.

Yet if we are to be true to the Scriptures themselves, next to these proof-texts we must also place the assertions that God 'desires everyone to be saved and to come to the knowledge of the truth' (1 Tim. 2.4), that Jesus 'is the atoning sacrifice for our sins, and not for ours only but also for the sins of the whole world' (1 John 2.2), and that 'the grace of God has appeared, bringing salvation to all' (Titus 2.11). We might note also, among other germane passages, some of Christ's own judgements on people's fitness to enter his kingdom: a Roman centurion (Matt. 8.5–13), a dissolute son (Luke 15.13–32), a destitute and sore-ridden beggar

(Luke 16.20–31), a crucified bandit (Luke 23.39–43), those who spend their time visiting prisoners and welcoming strangers (Matt. 25.31–46) – all fare rather better than 'many' who not only call out 'Lord, Lord', but have even prophesied, cast out demons, and worked miracles in his name (Matt. 7.21–22). There is nothing in these texts that explicitly touches on the salvation of *atheists* specifically: not least because, as previously mentioned, atheism in our modern sense was likely a wholly foreign concept to the biblical authors. Nevertheless, they ought to make us wary about feeling too sure about who – *in God's eyes* (which, it is always worth reminding ourselves, are the only eyes that ultimately matter here) – is 'in' and who is 'out'.

Christians, however, are warned to 'work out your own salvation with fear and trembling' (Phil. 2.12). That is to say, they should, without abandoning hope (cf. Rom. 8.24), be very conscious that their ultimate salvation is by no means a foregone conclusion. And since that is true of those who have supposedly 'clothed' themselves with Christ (Gal. 3.27), then it could be thought that even venturing an opinion, however tentative, as to the possible salvation of non-Christians is foolhardy in the extreme. And silence might be especially wise, given the apparently ambivalent, at-once-pessimistic-and-tantalizingly-hopeful, scriptural witness outlined above. It is better, perhaps, to say nothing, rather than risk leading people astray on so serious a topic – one that is, in the fullest senses of the words, a matter of life and death. Why not confidently echo Abraham's question, 'Shall not the Judge of all the earth do what is just?' (Gen. 18.25), and leave it at that?

Tempting though that solution is, the salvation or damnation of non-Christians in general, and (increasingly) of atheists in particular, is an urgent question both pastorally and apologetically, and one requiring a 'proper' (if prudently tentative and cautious) answer. On the one hand, the perceived exclusiveness, arrogance and unfairness of Christianity's understanding of 'who can be saved' is a frequent theme of unbelievers' critiques, and is often cited as giving the lie to Christians' affirmations of a loving God who is 'rich in mercy' (Eph. 2.4). On the other, the fear of automatic damnation for one's unbelieving friends, relatives and other loved ones, as well as for complete strangers, is one that weighs heavily – as it should do – on the minds of a vast number of Christians. As such, this is undoubtedly the most profound question that contemporary unbelief, and its inexorable growth, throws up for Christian theology.

Without becoming too mired in technical details, I want to trace a cautiously positive answer to this chapter's title question, avoiding the twin dangers of pessimism and presumption. We need not be too pessimistic, since there are ample resources within both Scripture and tradition to allow us, at the very least, to *hope* that atheists can indeed be saved. But likewise, we must not be presumptuous: multiple cautions of Scripture, not least that 'the gate is narrow and the road is hard that leads to life, and there are few who find it' (Matt. 7.14), are not lightly to be set aside.

Socrates and the Queen of Sheba

Though we're interested here in atheists, it is nonetheless true that much of what comes under this topic applies equally to the salvation of non-Christians in general. That is not true of every point: as we shall see, the possibility of salvation for atheists raises particular questions that do not occur when considering the salvation of non-Christian theists (and vice versa). Nevertheless, there is a good degree of overlap, especially on some of the biggest and most foundational issues.

In general terms, therefore, it will be salutary to note that the Christian Scriptures and tradition recognize not merely that a great many non-Christians are (or will be) saved, but moreover that a good number of them are even bona fide saints. The most obvious category of these is the 'holy ones' of the Old Testament. Jesus states categorically that 'many will come from east and west and will eat with Abraham and Isaac and Jacob in the kingdom of heaven' (Matt. 8.11), and Moses and Elijah appear at his Transfiguration in all three of the Synoptic Gospels. Crucially, the Old Testament saints include Gentiles as well as Jews. Jesus himself affirms that the Queen of Sheba will be one of the judges in the last days, along with the people of Nineveh (Matt. 12.41–42), and the Christian tradition has long accorded saintly status to, among others, Abel, Enoch, Noah and Job, all of whom lived either before, or otherwise outside of, both of the Old and New covenants.

In the early patristic period, moreover, other candidates were sometimes proffered even from beyond the bounds of the Old Testament. Our second-century friend Justin Martyr, for instance, was convinced that prior to the incarnation the Word was active within 'every race of men', and that everyone among them who lived 'reasonably' (or 'according to the Word')[1] was a kind of proto-Christian. He specifically mentions here those who 'have been thought

---

1 The Greek word *logos* can carry a huge range of meanings, including 'wisdom', 'word' (as it is normally translated in the prologue to John) and 'reason'. This allows Justin to make a play on 'according to reason' ('reasonably') and 'according to the Word', which unfortunately doesn't translate very well into English.

atheists (*atheoi*); as, among the Greeks, Socrates and Heraclitus, and men like them', while also remarking that there are so 'many others' that recounting them all would be 'tedious' (*First Apology*, 46).[2] Elsewhere, and interestingly, it is clear that Justin includes among such people 'not only philosophers and scholars . . . but also artisans and people entirely uneducated, despising both glory, and fear, and death' (*Second Apology*, 10). Admittedly, Justin's sanguineness has not been universally affirmed either by other early Fathers or by later theologians. That said, he is by no means a lone voice crying in the wilderness either. On the eve of the Reformation, for example, Erasmus could happily write (in his 1522 dialogue *The Godly Feast*), 'St Socrates, pray for us!', and 'perhaps the Spirit of Christ is more widespread than we understand and the company of saints includes many not in our calendar'.[3]

Inculpable ignorance

It will not have escaped your notice that all the people mentioned above lived *before* the incarnation. Hence they also lived before Christ's proclamation of the kingdom, his sending out of the apostles to 'make disciples of all nations' (Matt. 28.19), and his delineations of the seeming 'criteria' for salvation quoted in this chapter's opening paragraph. For example, the stringent insistence that 'The

---

2 This and all other quotations from Justin's writings may be found in Alexander Roberts and James Donaldson (eds), 1996, *The Ante-Nicene Fathers, Volume I: The Apostolic Fathers – Justin Martyr – Irenaeus*, Edinburgh: T & T Clark.

3 Erasmus Desiderius, [1522] 1997, *The Collected Works of Erasmus: Colloquies*, Toronto: University of Toronto Press, pp. 192, 194.

one who believes and is baptized will be saved; but the one who does not believe will be condemned' (Mark 16.16) *immediately* follows the injunction to 'Go into all the world and proclaim the good news to the whole creation' (16.15). Needless to say, it is rather hard to believe in the good news, and be baptized on its account, several centuries before the news itself has even happened, let alone been proclaimed. It is not that Moses, the Queen of Sheba or Justin's 'reasonable' Greeks had heard and rejected the gospel. They had not, and could not have, even encountered it. To use a piece of theological jargon, it can be said that they were *inculpably ignorant* of the gospel; that is, not only had they not heard it, but it wasn't their – or anyone else's – fault.

If Moses and the Queen of Sheba can be saved (as Jesus thinks), or if Socrates can (as Justin does), then they are able to be saved *despite* not having possessed an explicit faith in Christ and his gospel, or having been baptized – at least not during their lives on earth. That does not mean, of course, that everyone who lived before Christ gets a kind of 'get out of gaol free' card. As we shall see in the following sections, there is rather more to be said on this score. However, it is clear that their inculpable ignorance excuses them, at least to some degree, from the obligations incumbent upon those people living much later, who *have been* properly evangelized.

Now, this is an insight of crucial importance. In the first place it can certainly be argued that some of Christian history's most rigorous-sounding pronouncements on the non-salvation of non-Christians – normally summed up by the in itself perfectly correct patristic maxim, *Extra Ecclesiam nulla salus* ('Outside the Church, no salvation') – are based on the assumption that inculpable ignorance was, since soon after the incarnation, no longer a genuine possibility. By the early medieval period, for instance, it was widely thought that the good news had been preached, and preached well and convincingly, to all people. Thus anyone who *wasn't* a Christian must have actively rejected it, wilfully, culpably and in full knowledge of what they were doing. (Psychologically, it was probably very easy for medieval Europeans to assume that *all* Jews – traditionally vilified and the subject of pogroms every time there was a drought or famine – and *all* Muslims – widely regarded as 'stealers' of the Holy Land – fitted this category.) Over the centuries, however, it has become clear that this kind of blanket assumption is scarcely justified. Most significantly, the great geographical discoveries of the fifteenth century onwards made it quite plain that, even a millennium and a half after the incarnation, the gospel evidently *hadn't* yet been proclaimed 'to the whole creation'. Furthermore, as European missionaries set about trying to rectify this – not always with the highest of intentions and accompanied by brutal conquistadors – it rapidly became clear that simply being *told about* the gospel in a cursory fashion, especially by people seemingly more interested in stealing one's land and enslaving one's family, didn't necessarily constitute *evangelization* in the full and proper sense. That is to say, the idea began to dawn, albeit very slowly, that inculpable ignorance might well apply even to people who lived in the Christian era, and even to those who had 'heard' the gospel.

Returning now to our real topic of 'Can atheists be saved?', recall that the entire last chapter was devoted to just a small selection of the ways in which Christians *themselves*, 'by neglecting education in the faith, teaching false doctrine, or through defects in their own religious, moral or social lives . . . may be said rather more to conceal

than reveal the true countenance of God and of religion'
(*Gaudium et Spes*, 19). Given this, consider the possibility
that at least some of today's unbelievers can be considered
'inculpably ignorant' of the gospel. That is, despite having 'heard' the good news of Jesus Christ, a wide range of
social, cultural, moral and/or intellectual factors – some of
them no doubt the fault of believers – have prevented them
from ever properly *hearing* it, in a way that would obli-
gate them to accept.[4] (Think, for example, of how hollow
and unpersuasive even the most tightly argued and fault-
lessly presented piece of apologetics might sound against a
backdrop of constant reports of 'paedophile priests', institutional cover-ups etc.) John Sanders states this basic point
very well:

> I would also include among the unevangelized those
> who have been driven away from Christ not by the gos-
> pel but by the poor testimony or lifestyle of professing
> Christians. Our bigotry and greed, for instance, may
> prevent others from genuinely perceiving God's grace.
> Finally, I would argue that not all those who have heard
> a recitation of 'gospel facts' have thereby come to under-
> stand the gospel. There is more to evangelism than just
> transferring information.[5]

Admittedly, we have come a long way here in just a short
space: from Socrates and the Queen of Sheba being chrono-
logically incapable of hearing the gospel, to the New World

---

4 Tentatively, we might speculate that this could just as well apply to
some who have been brought up as Christians and even been baptized,
confirmed, first communicated, married in a Christian church etc.

5 John Sanders, 1990, *No Other Name: Can Only Christians Be
Saved?*, London: SPCK, p. 15 n. 2.

natives being geographically incapable of it, to today's unbelievers arguably being, not incapable, but what one might describe as culturally predisposed against *really* hearing it. Nevertheless, if the basic argument here – which I have stated more fully elsewhere[6] – is sound, then we have made an important first step in tracing the *possibility* of salvation for contemporary atheists.

Faith and baptism

It is important to realize, however, that the early theologians did not think that the Queen of Sheba, Abraham, Moses or Socrates were saved *merely because* of their inculpable ignorance. Not having heard the gospel is not, and never will be, a means of salvation. (If it was, then proclaiming the gospel to the hitherto unevangelized would make no sense whatsoever, since it would strip them of their 'automatic' salvation.) That is because, according to classical Christian theology, faith, baptism and the Church are not understood to be arbitrarily imposed 'hurdles' to beatitude, such that they can be dispensed with in certain circumstances. Strictly speaking, therefore, these conditions apply just as much to the inculpably ignorant as they do to those who have been properly evangelized: Jesus is 'the way, and the truth, and the life' for *everyone*, whether they (could) know about it or not. Despite being blamelessly unevangelized, Socrates, the Sheban Queen and perhaps some of our own unbelieving friends, still have a need

---

6 Stephen Bullivant, 2012, *The Salvation of Atheists and Catholic Dogmatic Theology*, Oxford: Oxford University Press, pp. 131–46.

for Christ, and thus for faith and baptism, in order 'to be saved and to come to the knowledge of the truth'.

How they might be able to fulfil these needs is, to some degree, an open question. There are a number of options on the theological table, none of which perhaps is wholly perfect. Here though, we will concentrate on just the proposed 'solutions' that have, historically speaking, been the most significant.

Let us begin by considering the need for *faith*. Think back to Justin Martyr's appeal to 'the Word of whom every race have been partakers' (*First Apology*, 46). For Justin, all those 'by human birth, more ancient than Christ' (*Second Apology*, 10), and who lived 'by the knowledge and contemplation of the . . . Word' (*Second Apology*, 8) have, albeit without knowing it, exhibited a kind of Christian faith. Evidently, this could not have been the explicit faith demanded of one who has been evangelized (cf. Mark 16.15–16). Yet according to Justin, this type of faith (though he does not use the term directly) is a real one nonetheless. This fact he considers proven by the willingness of figures such as Socrates to go to their deaths rather than renounce the ideals that they had staked their lives on (*Second Apology*, 10). Developing this idea, Justin affirms that Christ was therefore 'partially known even by Socrates' (*Second Apology*, 10).

This kind of appeal to some form of 'partial' – or, in more modern terms, 'implicit', 'anonymous' or 'unconscious' – faith has proven beguiling to several theologians over the centuries. And indeed, such moves gain a degree of scriptural support from Paul's appeals (as discussed briefly in the Introduction) to those Gentiles who have 'what the law requires . . . written on their hearts' (Rom. 2.15) and who worship 'the unknown God' (Acts 17.23). Such people, it would seem, not only live in accordance with God's laws but even worship the Most True God himself, despite being (presumably inculpably) unaware of these facts.[7] Traditionally, theologians have appealed to Hebrews 11.6 here – 'And without faith it is impossible to please God, for whoever would approach him must believe that he exists and that he rewards those who seek him' – with the assumption being that in this 'minimum' a genuine faith in the true God and his providential concern for humanity (and hence of the incarnation, crucifixion, resurrection, etc.) is, or at least might be, implicit. That is not, however, of any great help to our inculpably ignorant atheists, since it is precisely a belief that God 'exists' that they lack. Justin, however, is rather less precise in his criteria. For him, faithful, if unknowing, devotion to Christ is exhibited by those who live 'a reasonable and earnest life, and shun vice' (Second Apology, 8). Recent theologians have been even more creative in identifying possible proxies, implying (however indirectly) authentic faith. The French theologian Yves Congar is perhaps worth quoting at length on this score:

> And all the while there is the mass of men who know nothing of God, or whose knowledge is as good as nothing, who give the word 'God' meanings that are absurd, and sometimes repulsive . . . Their meeting with God could take place under the form of one of those master-words that stand for a transcendent absolute to which they may have given their love, words that are often written with a capital letter: Duty, Peace, Justice, Brotherhood, yes, and Humanity, Progress, Welfare, and

---

7 It is important to note here that Paul evidently did *not* think that worshippers of the 'unknown God' were thereby without need of evangelization. This is a point to which we shall return in Chapter 6.

yet others. People often give themselves to these ideals at the cost of their own personal interests and comfort, at the cost of themselves, and even sometimes of life. Is that not true love? But there is one thing that is privileged to be a paradoxical sign of God, in relation to which men are able to manifest their deepest commitment – our Neighbour. The sacrament of our Neighbour![8]

Claims such as these are not, it is true, without their difficulties. It might be questioned, for example, just how elastic the notion of an implicit faith can be without it snapping altogether. It can also been argued that there is perhaps something arrogant in Christians claiming as their own all that is good in the world, as with Justin's claiming as 'Christians' all virtuous people of the past, and even going so far as to say, 'Whatever things were rightly said among all men, are the property of us Christians' (*Second Apology*, 13). Nevertheless, this tradition perhaps has enough strength behind it for us to *begin* to conceive how a genuine faith might be present within at least some inculpably ignorant atheists. As I have already said, this is not the only possible option. For example, a number of theologians have instead favoured post-mortem solutions of one sort or another (which are also not without their theological difficulties and challenges). Thus far, however, it is the 'implicit faith' approach that has been most widely viewed as the most plausible option for grounding Christian *hope* on this score.

What, though, are we to make of the necessity of baptism? It is one thing to imagine someone having a faith in Christ of which he or she is not (and perhaps could not be) aware. It is

---

8 Yves Congar, 1961, *The Wide World My Parish*, trans. Donald Attwater, London: Darton, Longman & Todd, p. 124.

another thing entirely seriously to imagine his or her having received baptism without knowing it too. But that is precisely what the classical Christian understanding of salvation demands. Or rather, and more promisingly, it demands that he or she has received the sacramental 'effect' *ordinarily* conferred by being either immersed in, or sprinkled with, water by someone saying, 'I baptize you in the name of the Father, and of the Son, and of the Holy Spirit.'

Already in the early Christian centuries, it was believed that if a catechumen were, say, run over by a chariot on the way to being baptized, then his or her *desire* for baptism would suffice – and God, who is not after all a prisoner of the Church, would be able to supply the rest. Being martyred for the faith was also considered as providing a 'baptism of blood' for those not already baptized, and even already baptized martyrs were commonly described as receiving 'a second baptism'. Tertullian, writing in the early third century, thus describes martyrdom as 'the baptism which both stands in lieu of [baptism with water] when that has not been received, and restores it when lost' (*On Baptism*, 16).[9] Since it was a fairly common practice within the early Church to hold off one's baptism until late in life – for instance, St Ambrose, upon being elected as bishop of Milan by popular acclaim, had first to be baptized before being ordained and consecrated – the pastoral and theological problem posed by the sudden death of a sincere, holy but not yet baptized member of 'the household of faith' can scarcely have been uncommon.

But this did not only apply to explicit members of the Christian community. If baptism, in some form, is indeed

---

9 Quoted from Alexander Roberts and James Donaldson (eds), 1996, *The Ante-Nicene Fathers, Volume 3: Latin Christianity: Its Founder, Tertullian; I. Apologetic; II. Anti-Marcion; III. Ethical*, Edinburgh: T & T Clark, p. 677.

absolutely necessary for salvation – as Jesus, for one, seems to think that it is – then it follows that all those who are saved must receive it, *in some form*. Naturally, this includes all those who lived before Christ whom we have already mentioned. It also includes, at the very least, a number of others who lived at the same time as he did, including the Holy Innocents (Matt. 2.16–18) and the crucified thief whom Jesus himself assures 'Truly, this day you will be with me in paradise' (Luke 23.43). And again, ever creative, the early Fathers had a number of suggestions for quite how all this might be possible. The Holy Innocents, having been killed 'on account of' Christ, were venerated as martyrs, thus receiving a baptism of blood. Writing at the turn of the third century, St Clement of Alexandria imagined that, having descended to the dead on Holy Saturday, Jesus personally baptized the righteous Jews of the Old Testament, while the apostles, upon their own deaths, did the honours for their Gentile contemporaries. From around the same time, *The Martyrdom of Sts Perpetua and Felicity* (which also describes martyrdom as 'a second baptism') even suggests that a saint's fervent prayers are able to bring a dead relative's soul to both baptism and eternal life. Meanwhile, St Augustine – as firm a believer in the necessity for baptism for salvation as the Church has ever produced – thought that circumcision functioned as a proxy for baptism for the saints of the Old Testament (though what sufficed for either the women and/or those outside the Abrahamic covenant among them, he does not state). He also argued that the water issuing from Christ's pierced side would have been sufficient for Luke's repentant thief.[10]

---

10 On Augustine (and much else), see Jeffrey A. Trumbower, 2001, *Rescue from the Dead: The Posthumous Salvation of Non-Christians in Early Christianity*, Oxford: Oxford University Press.

My purpose in offering these disparate examples is not to argue that all – or necessarily any – of the above give us the true means by which the Most True God actually does bring baptism to those who have, for certain reasons, been prevented from receiving it in the normal and normative way. And even excusing their at times ingenious implausibility, judging by the standards of later orthodoxy, some of them can be found wanting in very serious ways. Rather, my point is simply to make plain that even among the earliest – and in the case of Augustine at least, most uncompromising – Christian theologians, there is a remarkable openness to the idea that baptism, though necessary in itself, need not *always* be conferred in the usual way. This basic insight, implicit within the rococo fecundity of the above hypotheses, is expressed rather neatly by Thomas Aquinas: 'God has not bound his power to the sacraments, so as not to be able, outside of the sacraments, to confer the effect of the sacraments' (*Summa theologiae*, III, q. 64, a. 7). Incidentally, it is this basic principle that partly grounds the Christian hope for infants, including the unborn, who die without baptism.[11]

It is clear then that, as with the requirement of faith, the Christian tradition already contains a number of theological resources to help us start to conceive how contemporary atheists *might* receive the effect of baptism, even if they have never received sacramental baptism. That said, it is worth pointing out that a significant number of today's atheists *have been* baptized. While this rather complicates matters, if some of the arguments sketched out above are correct,

---

11 See International Theological Commission, 2007, *The Hope of Salvation for Infants who Die Without Being Baptised*, London: Catholic Truth Society.

then it is indeed nevertheless possible that they remain inculpably ignorant of the gospel of Christ. For those who haven't been baptized in the normal way, however, then on this score their situation is no more problematic than that of any other non-Christian. Let us put it like so: if baptism is necessary for salvation (as, based on Scripture and tradition, it would certainly seem to be), and if Noah or the Queen of Sheba are saved (as, based on Scripture and tradition, they certainly seem to be), then there *must* be some 'extra-ordinary' means by which God is able to bring this about it. As we have seen, even focusing on the early Church alone, there has been no shortage of *suggestions* as to how this might be done. These are a mixed bag, and some are admittedly more plausible and satisfactory than others. But even if none is correct, Christians may still be confident that the Holy Trinity has some means up its celestial sleeve. That is to say (albeit a little irreverently), if St Peter were to meet a virtuous, 'reasonable' in Justin's sense, inculpably ignorant atheist at the Pearly Gates with the question, 'And who do you think you are, *the Queen of Sheba?*' then in one sense at least, he might not be so far wide of the mark.

'Every knee shall bow to me, and every tongue shall give praise'?

Throughout all of this chapter I have been advising caution. It is true that the classical Christian tradition affirms, unambiguously, that a significant number of non-Christians can and will be saved. It is also true that there are sufficient theological resources within this polyphonic tradition to suggest ways in which modern non-believers may well be included among them. So much so that at the

Second Vatican Council (1962–5) the Roman Catholic Church declared explicitly for the first time that those who 'without fault, have not yet arrived at an express recognition of God' – that is, are inculpably ignorant atheists – are *able to be* saved (*Lumen Gentium*, 16). The possibility is assured, and it is this possibility that I have done my best to flesh out in the above paragraphs. *Actuality* is, however, a rather different question entirely. While, on this point too, I have raised what I take to be legitimate grounds for *hope*, how many atheists will actually be saved – one? forty four? eight billion? – is a question without answer this side of the day when 'the Queen of the South will rise up at the judgement' (Matt. 12.42). Those familiar with the rest of that quotation will be aware that, again according to Jesus, our friend from Sheba is not necessarily a lenient judge.

It is with due fear and trembling, then, that we may now broach a very different idea concerning the salvation of, well, *everyone*. This is the theory that, ultimately, *all people* – Christians, Jews, Buddhists, atheists, saints, sinners, Nobel Prize winners, genocide-perpetrators and literally everyone else – will, no doubt in many cases following a long process of purification and transformation, hear Christ say, 'Come, you that are blessed by my Father, inherit the kingdom prepared for you from the foundation of the world' (Matt. 25.34).

Although very much of a minority report, variants of this basic theme have proven stubbornly persistent ideas throughout Christian history. In the early Church, for instance, Peter's assertion in Acts that Christ 'must remain in heaven, until the time of universal restoration (*apokatastasis*) that God announced long ago through his holy prophets' (3.21) influenced the view that all souls would one day be restored, or 'reconciled' to Christ. This doctrine of *apokatastasis* has been ascribed to a number of early theologians – though how accurately was often a subject of keen debate, as it still is today – including St Clement of Alexandria, Origen of Alexandria (whose posthumous condemnation rested largely on his alleged support for the doctrine), and St Gregory of Nyssa.

To give a rather different example, from another time and place entirely, somewhat similar theologies developed in strands of American Calvinism beginning in the eighteenth century. These found their most famous expression from the late nineteenth century onwards in certain communities of the Primitive Baptist Church in Virginia, Tennessee and Kentucky, leading to these 'no-hellers' (as they came to be called) formally splitting off in 1925. These Primitive Baptist groups – who presumably aren't the same ones that Washington Phillips had in mind (see Chapter 3!) – continue to this day. Elsewhere in modern Calvinist theology, the Swiss theologian Karl Barth, considered by many to be the greatest theologian of the twentieth century, is often identified – although, as with the early theologians, not uncontroversially – as having affirmed, at least implicitly, universal salvation.

In recent times, however, universalism is perhaps most often associated with two writers and books: the Swiss Catholic theologian Hans Urs von Balthasar and *Dare We Hope "That All Men Be Saved"?*, and the American non-denominational 'megachurch' pastor Rob Bell and *Love Wins*. While starting from very different places, and differing in certain other respects too, both authors stress that against every 'restrictive' scriptural text concerning who will be saved, one can place an equally authoritative one, emphasizing God's infinite love, mercy and desire that none shall be lost. A small sample of each kind was given in the introduction to this chapter. Given this tension present in Scripture itself, Balthasar insists that it cannot simply be resolved by arbitrarily privileging the first set over the other:

> It is not for man, who is *under* judgment, to construct syntheses here, and above all none of such a kind as to subsume one series of statements under the other, practically emasculating the universalist ones because he believes himself to have 'certain knowledge' of the potency of the first.[12]

Writing in a slightly different context, Bell makes a broadly similar point: 'those are tensions we are free to leave fully intact. We don't need to resolve them or answer them because we can't, and so we simply respect them, creating space for the freedom that love requires.'[13]

For both writers, this tension – and specifically the refusal to collapse it one way or the other – opens up the possibility of *hoping* that, ultimately, all will be saved. This is a point that Balthasar, in particular, is keen to stress: 'I never spoke of certainty but rather of hope'[14] – and he is happy to admit that the possibility also remains open for hoping the opposite too. As he laconically puts it: 'I do not wish to contradict anyone who, as a Christian, cannot be happy without denying the universality of hope to us so that he can be certain of his full hell.'[15] Concerning *how* the hope that all will be saved might be fulfilled, both Bell and

---

12 Hans Urs von Balthasar, 1988, *Dare We Hope That "All Men Be Saved"?*, trans. David Kipp and Lothar Krauth, San Francisco, CA: Ignatius Press, p. 23.

13 Rob Bell, 2011, *Love Wins: At the Heart of Life's Big Questions*, New York: Collins, p. 115.

14 Balthasar, *Dare We Hope*, p. 18.

15 Balthasar, *Dare We Hope*, p. 187.

Balthasar emphasize God's stated desire for 'everyone to be saved and to come to the knowledge of the truth' (1 Tim. 2.4), as is also expressed in such a familiar passage as: 'God did not send the Son into the world to condemn the world, but in order that the world might be saved through him' (John 3.17). For both writers, the central question here, as neatly expressed by Bell, is effectively, 'Does God get what God wants?'[16] While neither denies the reality and gravity of human sin and freedom – and thus the capacity of human beings to *refuse* God's offer of grace – Balthasar and Bell concur in their depiction of a God who himself refuses to give up and who, like Francis Thompson's Hound of Heaven, relentlessly pursues his quarry 'with unhurrying chase, and unperturbed pace'.[17] Bell asks: 'Which is stronger and more powerful, the hardness of the human heart, or God's unrelenting, infinite, expansive love?'[18]

The hopeful vision expressed here is, indeed, an attractive one. Given the serious thinkers who have espoused it (or something very like), and the diverse theological contexts out of which it has arisen, it is not an idea that ought to be dismissed lightly. Its basic thrust is, moreover, rather more theologically mainstream than it is sometimes supposed to be. For example, large numbers of Catholics the world over pray the 'Fátima prayer' on a regular basis, normally as one of the prayers added after each decade of the rosary. Its final petition to 'my Jesus' requests that he 'lead *all souls to heaven*, especially those with most need of thy

---

16 Bell, *Love Wins*, p. 95.

17 Francis Thompson, [1893], 'The Hound of Heaven', in Theodore E. James (ed.), 1997, *The Heart of Catholicism: Essential Writings of the Church from St. Paul to John Paul II*, Huntington, IN: Our Sunday Visitor, pp. 517–22, at p. 518.

18 Bell, *Love Wins*, p. 109.

mercy' (emphasis added). The most natural reading of this is that it evinces at least a hope for universal salvation.

Evidently, if all souls will ultimately be saved, then *ipso facto* this encompasses all atheist souls as well. This need not conflict with the ideas outlined in our preceding sections. Presumably, faith, baptism and the involvement of the Church are just as necessary if all will be saved, as they are if only some will be. The role of various post-mortem means of bringing these about will, though, probably take on a greater significance. This is a huge and contentious topic in itself, which is why it was only touched upon briefly above. Both Balthasar and Bell do, though, rely heavily on the possibility of after-death conversion to a God who is willing to play the 'long game' in reconciling all things to himself. (This is an idea which, for various reasons, has tended not to find much favour in the mainstream theological tradition.)

As it happens, in *The Brothers Karamazov*, Dostoevsky – or, more accurately, a devil who may or may not be a hallucinatory symptom of Ivan's impending madness – offers us a very similar idea. He recounts the legend of a philosopher who 'rejected all – laws, conscience, faith, and, above all, the future life.'

> He died and thought he'd go straight into darkness and death, but no – there was the future life before him. He was amazed and indignant. 'This', he said, 'goes against my convictions.' So for that he was sentenced . . . to walk in darkness a quadrillion kilometres (we also use kilometres now), and once he finished that quadrillion, the doors of paradise would be opened to him and he would be forgiven everything.[19]

---

19 Fyodor Dostoevsky, [1880] 2004, *The Brothers Karamazov*, trans. Richard Pevear and Larissa Volokhonsky, London: Vintage, p. 643.

There follows a brief, philosophical and funny exchange between Ivan and the devil, before he reaches his conclusion:

> The moment the doors of paradise were opened and he went in, before he had even been there two seconds . . . he exclaimed that for those two seconds it would be worth walking not just a quadrillion kilometres, but a quadrillion quadrillion, even raised to the quadrillionth power! In short, he sang 'Hosannah' and oversweetened it so much, that some persons there, of a nobler cast of mind, did not even want to shake hands with him at first: he jumped over to the conservatives a bit too precipitously.

Ivan's devil ends by emphasizing, once again, that this is merely 'a legend. Take it for what it's worth.'[20]

Without *in any way* being so dismissive of the Christian hope for universal salvation, it would be negligent to conclude this section without freely admitting that, for all its beguilement, there remain a number of huge question marks over it – not least, as our authors freely admit, the strong testimony of Scripture (and especially, one might add, in the sayings of Jesus himself) in the other direction. Indeed, as John Henry Newman once wrote in one of his Anglican parish sermons, commenting on Christ's assertion that 'many are called, but few are chosen' (Matt. 22.14):

> Of course we must not press the words of Scripture; we do not know the exact meaning of the word 'chosen'; we do not know what is meant by being saved 'so as by fire'; we do not know what is meant by 'few'. But still the few can never mean the many; and to be called without

---

20 Dostoevsky, *Brothers Karamazov*, p. 644.

being chosen cannot but be a misery.[21] If hope is indeed justified, then complacency is not.

Conclusion

As stated above, the question of salvation is indubitably the weightiest of all the topics treated in this book. This is not surprising, since it is also the weightiest of all the topics treated in Christian theology as a whole. (We should not forget, for example, that all the seemingly arcane trinitarian and christological disputes of the patristic period were, at root, motivated by precisely this issue.) Here, *even more* than in all the other chapters, we have barely been able to scratch the surface. Nevertheless, some important things have, I hope, been achieved.

The first has been to sketch out the biblical and traditional rationale for comprehending how, within orthodox Christian theology, the salvation of atheists can be understood and explored. This involves principally the notion of inculpable ignorance, as well as identifying some extraordinary means by which virtuous non-believers might fulfil the requirements of faith and baptism. As outlined above, much of the foundational thinking work here has already been done for us by the early Church Fathers, not least by one of this book's two 'patrons', St Justin Martyr.

The second has been to introduce some of the key issues surrounding the hope for universal salvation. Drawing particularly on the very-different-but-oddly-similar writings of

---

21 John Henry Newman, [1837] 1987, *Parochial and Plain Sermons*, San Francisco, CA: Ignatius Press, p. 1128.

Rob Bell and Hans Urs von Balthasar, and with a little help from our other patron Fyodor Dostoevsky, I have tried to highlight some of the main grounds for this hope, while at the same time cautioning against what one might call 'salvational nonchalance' (while, I might add, in no way accusing Bell, Balthasar or Dostoevsky of this).

I spoke in this chapter's introduction about the need to steer a course between pessimism – 'all non-Christians are damned!' – and presumption – 'we needn't worry, that whole "narrow gate" thing was just Jesus being rhetorical!' Salvation is, after all, a serious matter. And in thinking about it as Christians, as St Paul well knew, there is ample room for *both* 'fear and trembling' *and* a conviction that 'in hope we were saved'. We will do well to keep this in mind when we come to Chapter 6. Before that, however, it is time to discuss dialogue.

5

Dialogue with unbelievers

Dialogue – speaking and *listening* to one another – has, particularly over the course of the past century, become a major feature of the Christian landscape. Pretty well every major denomination devotes a significant amount of time, effort, money and thought to engaging and co-operating with both other types of Christian and members of non-Christian religions. One need not look far on the websites of most denominations, dioceses or even individual churches to uncover a wealth of initiatives and endeavours, ranging from the very local (e.g. speakers at parish coffee mornings) to the truly global (like the World Council of Churches founded in 1948, and the huge interfaith gatherings held at Assisi since 1986). Genuine dialogue is never easy, least of all on those issues most in need of conversation and, if not actual agreement, then at least greater understanding. Despite this, both inter-Christian and interfaith engagements have indeed borne notable fruits, as for instance in the vastly improved relations between Christians and Jews in the wake of the Shoah or in the historic agreement on the doctrine of justification reached by the Catholic Church and the World Lutheran Federation of 1999.

Rather less known, and certainly less practised, than either its ecumenical or interreligious varieties is dialogue with unbelievers and/or the non-religious in general. This would seem to be a significant omission. After all, unbelief and non-religiosity are major features of the cultures and societies where 'dialogue with the Other'[1] has been received most enthusiastically by the Christian communities. On a global scale, moreover, a recent estimate places 'non-believers in God' as the world's fourth most numerous (non)religious grouping, behind Christians, Muslims and Hindus. The same author notes that worldwide 'there are approximately 58 times as many atheists as there are Mormons, 41 times as many atheists as there are Sikhs, and twice as many atheists as there are Buddhists.'[2] Members of all three of these religions (along with many, many more) are, rightly enough, frequently engaged by dialogue-minded Christians of various stripes – far, far more frequently, it need hardly be said, than are unbelievers.

Challenge and opportunity

In part, the reasons for this are quite practical and mundane. As noted in Chapter 3, in most western countries the existence of significant and socially visible unbelieving populations is a comparatively recent phenomenon. Furthermore, being an atheist in itself does not make one an adherent of a particular belief-system or a member of a defined group.

---

1 David Tracy, 1990, *Dialogue with the Other: The Inter-Religious Dialogue*, Louvain: Peeters.

2 Phil Zuckerman, 2007, 'Atheism: Contemporary Numbers and Patterns', in Michael Martin (ed.), *The Cambridge Companion to Atheism*, New York: Cambridge University Press, pp. 47–65, at p. 55.

Being an atheist simply means that, for whatever reasons, one either believes that there is or are no God or gods ('positive atheism') or, at least, *lacks* a belief that there is/are ('negative atheism'). This means that atheism is compatible with a whole host of very different, and in some cases opposing, world views, not excluding some religious ones. It is also compatible with not really having much of a well-defined world view at all, or seeing the need for one. Obviously, finding legitimate representatives or spokespeople for 'atheists as a whole' is impossible. But that is not an excuse for not even trying; the same kind of problems can occur in finding *any* such dialogue partners. (Who, for example, can speak on behalf of 'all' Muslims, Jews or Christians?) While one obviously cannot enter into a meaningful dialogue with all unbelievers at once, the atheist landscape is not so chaotic that one cannot identify significant groups of (relatively) likeminded *types* of atheists – such as humanists or Marxists – or high-profile individuals with whose views many other atheists find an affinity. Not that all dialogue partners need to speak 'on behalf of' (in however loose a sense) a wider constituency. Indeed, it is probably the case that the most meaningful and revealing exchanges occur when people feel able to speak personally, *for* themselves alone, rather than feeling obliged faithfully to reflect or represent the views of others. An additional problem is that certain people or groups may not want to dialogue with certain other people or groups. Worthwhile dialogue requires trust, respect and a willingness to listen and learn. It may be that there are some atheists who do not trust, respect or have any desire to listen to or learn from Christians in general, or members of specific Christian groups. (Certainly, there are a great many Christians who feel that way about atheists, so we oughtn't to throw stones here.) If so, then fine: there is, after all, 'a time to keep silence, and a time to speak' (Eccles. 3.7). But this is a poor excuse to refrain from even issuing invitations.

Dialogue with atheists might actually prove easier, and more interesting, than dialogue with other groups. Unlike with ecumenical dialogue, there are no pressures for 'moving towards full communion' or reaching joint doctrinal agreements. There is no real need to reach any substantial 'agreements' at all. That is not to say there won't be significant areas of common ground or that new possibilities for practical collaboration won't emerge. But the fact remains that Christians and atheists *ought to* disagree, decisively and strongly, on many questions of significance. Indeed, it would be very strange and worrisome if they did not. As the atheist philosopher Michael Ruse has written recently:

The existence of the deity – to be a believer, a theist in some sense, or to be a non-believer, an atheist in some sense – is no mere matter of academic concern and interest. Nor is it something merely of moment for the hereafter, beyond the deaths of each and every one of us. A world with God and a world without God are two very different places, with very different meanings and obligations for us humans who occupy them. Humans created, loved, and supported by the deity are humans very different from those who wander alone, without external meaning or purpose, creating their own destinies.[3]

---

3 Stephen Bullivant and Michael Ruse, 2013, 'The Study of Atheism', in Stephen Bullivant and Michael Ruse (eds), *The Oxford Handbook of Atheism*, Oxford: Oxford University Press. Note that while this is taken from a jointly authored piece – and I fully agree with the sentiment expressed here – the precise words issued from Michael's keyboard rather than my own.

Neither a belief in the Most True God, nor a lack of belief in any God at all, 'leaves everything as it is'.[4] The decision between faith and unbelief is a momentous one, and has and ought to have important ramifications, both abstract and concrete. An authentic, frank dialogue between Christians and atheists should reflect this, and be all the more interesting and illuminating for it. In the words of Peter Hebblethwaite:

> Dialogue presupposes disagreement and distinction; otherwise it would be unnecessary. In dialogue one is trying to build a bridge. To do so one must be firmly planted *somewhere*, on one side. If, imperceptibly and unconsciously, one slides over to the other side there will be no bridge-building, only fusion becoming confusion.[5]

Developing this theme, in this chapter I would like to outline, in some detail, the potential benefits to both 'sides' from pursuing Christian–atheist dialogue in our contemporary, western context. As we shall see, there are currently promising signs of growth and vitality in this area. But before this, it should be both worthwhile and interesting to give a bit of background and history. For while dialoguing with unbelievers might *seem* to be a novel idea, to again quote from Ecclesiastes: 'there is nothing new under the sun. Is there a thing of which it is said, "See, this is new"? It has already been, in the ages before us' (1.9–10).

---

4 Ludwig Wittgenstein, [1953] 2009, *Philosophical Investigations*, trans. G. E. M. Anscombe, P. M. S. Hacker and Joachim Schulte, 4th edn, Oxford: Wiley-Blackwell, p. 55.

5 Peter Hebblethwaite, 1971, 'Brief Commentary on the Directory', in Peter Hebblethwaite (ed.), *Talking with Unbelievers (Part 2)*, Douglas: Times Longbook, pp. 137–45, at p. 139.

Everybody's talkin'

As we saw in Chapter 2, Dostoevsky's 1880 novel *The Brothers Karamazov* contains a lengthy episode in which the unbelieving Ivan and his novice monk brother Alyosha – like so many young people, before and since – sit discussing the big questions in a pub. The encounter is not, admittedly, the model of what a Christian–atheist dialogue might be, since the bulk of their conversation comprises two lengthy *mono*logues, delivered by Ivan, with only occasional interjections by Alyosha. But as a free and frank exchange of ideas, it is Christian–atheist dialogue all the same. And while a fictional example, the reader certainly gets the impression that this is a typical scene: 'All of young Russia is talking now only about eternal questions. Precisely now, just when all the old men have suddenly gotten into practical questions.'[6] Other examples of such low-key, 'everyday dialogue' between Christians and atheists occur elsewhere in nineteenth-century European literature – as, for instance, in Georg Büchner's 1835 play, *Danton's Death*, and in Ivan Turgenev's 1862 novel, *Fathers and Sons*. It seems probable that these are cases of art imitating life. As growing numbers began to regard themselves as unbelievers, and have the confidence to 'come out' at least to friends and family, it would only be natural that these kinds of conversations should arise. And indeed, this kind of informal exchange between those already joined by bonds of trust and respect – as opposed to formally organized 'Dialogues' in person or print – remains the most common and quite probably the most meaningful type of dialogue to this day.

---

6 Fyodor Dostoevsky, [1880] 2004, *The Brothers Karamazov*, trans. Richard Pevear and Larissa Volokhonsky, London: Vintage, p. 233.

Moving into the twentieth century, as unbelief increased, so too did the popularity of (typically) atheistic world views such as Marxism, humanism and existentialism. Accordingly, the opportunity for, and importance of, such grassroots dialogue grew with them. This was especially true in areas, chiefly in Europe, where Christians and Marxists routinely lived side by side. In industrial areas, for example, socially engaged Christians and union organizing socialists might naturally strike up a rapport. This is exactly what happened during the French 'priest-worker' experiment of the 1940s and 1950s, in which clerics, often Jesuits or Dominicans, went to work as miners, dockers and factory workers in order to reach the emerging 'missionary territories' among the working classes. In more rural areas, circumstance and necessity might perhaps draw a village's Catholic priest and Communist mayor into a lively, if uneasy, working relationship. Again from the realm of fiction, we find exactly such a friendly (and volatile) rivalry depicted in Giovanni Guareschi's much-loved *Don Camillo* stories, set in post-war northern Italy and inspired by real life.

In the 1930s, 1940s and 1950s, one also begins to find moves towards more formalized attempts at dialogue, this time among the intelligentsia. In spite or perhaps because of obvious tensions between Christians and communists elsewhere in the world (including elsewhere in Europe), the General Secretary of the French Communist Party in 1936, and the President of its Italian counterpart in 1954, proposed dialogue with their Catholic compatriots, resulting in a number of meetings. There was also a great deal of what one might call 'literary dialogue' – books and articles, written from both sides, and engaging with the other in a serious and deep (though by no means uncritical) way. Henri de Lubac's still-in-print *The Drama of Atheist*

Humanism – focusing on Marx, Feuerbach, Comte and Nietzsche (and also, like us, making much of Dostoevsky) – is probably the most significant of these, though there were many others.

Arguably the most remarkable encounter of this period, however, was indeed a genuinely face-to-face one. In 1948, the Dominicans of Latour-Maubourg, on the outskirts of Paris, invited the atheist philosopher Albert Camus to speak about his views of Christianity, especially in light of its alleged failings during the previous catastrophic decades. The entire lecture (or rather, as much of it has been published) is very much worth reading. Here, though, I wish to quote a lengthy passage from towards the beginning, since it outlines what I believe is a cardinal principle for all authentic dialogue. After thanking the friars for their kindness and 'intellectual generosity' in wanting to hear from 'a man who does not share your convictions', Camus promises:

> I shall not try to change anything that I think or anything that you think (insofar as I can judge of it) in order to reach a reconciliation that would be agreeable to all. On the contrary, what I feel like telling you today is that the world needs real dialogue, that falsehood is just as much the opposite of dialogue as silence, and that the only possible dialogue is the kind between people who remain what they are and speak their minds.[7]

This is the same point I made in introducing this chapter: the necessity of honest disagreement. This must not *prevent* areas

---

7 Albert Camus, [1948] 1964, 'The Unbeliever and Christians', in *Resistance, Rebellion and Death*, trans. Justin O'Brien, London: Hamish Hamilton, pp. 47–53, at p. 48.

of concord being discovered and built upon. But Christians and unbelievers ultimately cannot, and should not, agree on perhaps very many questions of real significance. As Camus puts it: 'I share with you the same revulsion from evil. But I do not share your hope, and I continue to struggle against this universe in which children suffer and die.'[8]

Dialogue with unbelievers really took off, in an organized way, in the 1960s and 1970s. In April 1965, Pope Paul VI founded a Secretariat for Non-believers, for the precise purpose of understanding and dialoguing with atheists. The time seems, moreover, to have been opportune. Within days of its having been rather quietly announced, the Director of the American Humanist Association wrote to the Secretariat's President, Cardinal König, not merely welcoming the idea but sending literature, inviting members of the new body to meet with thirty humanist groups in the Netherlands that July, and even declaring his 'admiration' for the late Pope John XXIII as 'this great model of humanity'.[9] A number of high-profile, international events soon followed, most notably a series of conferences focusing on Christian–Marxist dialogue held in Germany, Austria and Czechoslovakia. Participants at these included the prominent Marxist philosophers Ernst Bloch (whom we met briefly in Chapter 1), Milan Machoveč and Roger Garaudy, as well as Catholic

---

8 Camus, 'The Unbeliever', p. 50.

9 The document is held in the archives of the Pontifical Council for Culture, Vatican City. For the sake of scholarly form, the full details for the manuscript are as follows: *Archivio Segretariato per i Non-Credenti*. 167/820-910. 'Corrispondenza (Umanisti): 1965, 1966, 1967'; subfile '1965', f. 23: 'Letter from Tolbert H. McCarroll (Executive Director of the American Humanist Association, Yellow Springs, OH) to Cardinal Koenig, April 14 1965', Prot. 65/06, 2 pages.

and Protestant thinkers of such calibre as Karl Rahner, Yves Congar, Paul Ricœur and Jürgen Moltmann.

After a decade or so of considerable activity, however, the momentum began to fade. This was so for a number of reasons. Dialogue with (non) believers, and those willing to engage in it, had always been viewed with suspicion by people on both sides. While this had caused problems from the beginning,[10] as time went on, internal pressures began to mount. It also became increasingly difficult to find willing dialogue partners. Many of those originally involved moved on to other priorities, while the next generation of philosophers and theologians regarded Christian–atheist engagement as something that had been 'done already'. At least on the Christian side, this suspicion was galvanized by the dawning realization that with the advent of postmodernity, grand all-encompassing world views such as Marxism, existentialism and humanism (and indeed, Christianity) were losing their appeal for large swathes of people – an intuition seemingly confirmed by the rapid disintegration of the formerly monolithic Eastern Bloc towards the end of the 1980s. Against this backdrop, official dialogues between Christians and atheists – which, in practice, had almost always been with representatives of humanist and Marxist groups – not unnaturally would have seemed like a relic of a bygone age. It was not surprising, then, when in 1993 the Secretariat (renamed in 1988 as the Pontifical

---

10 To give just two examples: Roger Garaudy was expelled from the French Communist Party in 1968; in 1969, Giulio Girardi, a key member of the Secretariat and one of the 'ghost writers' of Vatican II's statement on atheism, was suspended from his professorship in Rome. It is also possible that the rise of Liberation Theology in the late 1960s caused, in certain Church quarters, further disquiet concerning the desirability of dialogue and co-operation between Christians and Marxists.

Council for Dialogue with Non-believers) was quietly amal-
gamated by Pope John Paul II into the Pontifical Council
for Culture, which he had founded a decade earlier.

This was not, however, the end of the road – far from it.
In the early 1990s, the kind of self-assured positive atheism ('atheism-with-a-capital-A') associated with Marxism
and existentialism may well have seemed on the way out.
By the mid-2000s, however, it was clear that reports of its
demise had been greatly exaggerated. The rise of the New
Atheism, beginning with Sam Harris' surprise bestseller *The
End of Faith* in 2004, is the most obvious example here.
But the New Atheism is itself part of a much broader and
deeper strengthening of unbelief, evident in many different
countries from the dawn of the twenty-first century (and
earlier). It is therefore not surprising that Christian–atheist
dialogue now seems on the verge of a second spring.

Pleasingly and healthily, this comes in a wide variety
of forms. At the more formal end of the spectrum, there
have been a number of well-publicized encounters between
leading theologians and atheist intellectuals. While he was
Archbishop of Canterbury, Rowan Williams held public conversations with Richard Dawkins and the novelist
Philip Pullman (author of the *His Dark Materials* tril-
ogy). There have also been thoughtful exchanges between
Catholic prelates and prominent unbelievers, not least the
hour-long discussion between Dawkins and Cardinal Pell,
the Archbishop of Sydney, on Australian television in April
2012.[11] In late 2009, Pope Benedict announced a new ini-
tiative aimed at fostering a 'dialogue with those to whom

---

11 At the time of writing, the full show can be watched at: www.
youtube.com/watch?v=tD1QHO_AVZA. See 'Further reading' for other
such encounters.

religion is something foreign, to whom God is unknown',[12] named 'The Court of the Gentiles', and entrusted to the Pontifical Council for Culture. High-profile events under this banner have already happened in Portugal, Italy, France and Sweden.

More promising still is the growing phenomenon of low-key, grassroots dialogue. A small amount of Googling turns up all manner of encounters, whether in person or online: regular Christian–atheist meet-up groups in US cities, one-off dialogues held in church halls or university chaplaincies, discussions held on internet messageboards, blogs co-authored by two dialogue partners, video 'conversations' between YouTube users and so on. These are instances of dialogue that – quite unlike public encounters between a Dawkins and a Williams or Pell – attract little fanfare, but that may ultimately prove all the more meaningful for the parties involved. Without tempting fate, it may well be that we are entering a new, creative and exciting age of Christian–atheist dialogue.

But what's the point?

That is all very well and good, but *why* do it in the first place? I suggested above that dialoguing with unbelievers might be easier and more interesting than dialoguing with other Christians, or members of other faiths, since the pressure is off in terms of feeling a need to reach concrete agreements. While that may be true, it is arguably the need or desire to reach such agreements, or to find new ways of living and working together, that makes such dialogue worthwhile in

---

12 See: www.vatican.va/holy_father/benedict_xvi/speeches/2009/december/documents/hf_ben-xvi_spe_20091221_curia-auguri_en.html.

the first place. Attempting to reach significant ecumenical agreements on issues of doctrine or liturgy is certainly hard work, but it is worth persevering with in order to make progress, however slowly, towards the goal 'that they may all be one' (John 17.21). Likewise, advancing mutual understanding and co-operation between Christians, Jews and Muslims is fraught with difficulties, but is crucial for – among other things – furthering peace and the common good. What, though, is the point of Christian–atheist dialogue? Obviously, there is the sheer interest and pleasure one can sometimes get from talking to new people, with different views from one's own. But to be fair, that is just as strong an argument for taking up birdwatching or line dancing as it is for seriously pursuing Christian–atheist exchange. In the remainder of this chapter, therefore, I would like to outline, in some detail, two specific kinds of benefit that may be had from such dialogue.

Both sides now

As discussed in Chapter 3, it is a common complaint among Christians that unbelievers – or at least a vocal subset of them – frequently harbour and spread misconceptions about Christianity's doctrines and history, along with damaging and baseless stereotypes about the intellectual and moral calibre of its adherents. If so, then dialogue offers an opportunity not just to counter these errors but to understand the reasons why they have arisen in the first place. If one feels that interpretations of Genesis 1, the theology of the Cross, the Galileo affair or the reasons why Christians perform good works are being misunderstood or misrepresented, then actually sitting down and discussing these issues is surely a mature and constructive way of giving 'an account of the hope that is in you' (1 Peter 3.15–16).

Since dialogue is a two-way street, this benefit accrues in both directions. Misconceiving and stereotyping are hardly the preserve of (some) non-believers, and as a group they have just as much right to feel aggrieved on this score. Atheists are often enough perceived as being unfeeling believers in 'nothing', leading meaningless lives, with no reason to be good and little to offer themselves or others in the face of life's trials. This is especially true in the comparative Christian stronghold of the United States of America. A famous 2006 study by sociologists at the University of Minnesota, for example, found that almost 40% of the thousands of Americans they interviewed felt that atheists 'do not agree with my vision of American society' (Muslims at 26% and homosexuals at 23% were the next most popular choices). Furthermore, almost half would disapprove if their son or daughter married an atheist (Muslims at 36% and African Americans at 27% came in second and third). Interestingly, the report's authors comment: 'We believe that in answering our questions about atheists, our survey respondents were not, on the whole, referring to actual atheists they had encountered, but were responding to "the atheist" as a boundary-marking cultural category.'[13] That is to say, these negative judgements were based not on any bad experiences with *actual* atheists but on a pervasive, symbolic stereotype of the unethical and unpatriotic non believer. This kind of stigma can have concrete ramifications, and there is a growing body of research

---

13 Penny Edgell et al., 2006, 'Atheists as "Other": Moral Boundaries and Cultural Membership in American Society', *American Sociological Review* 71/2, pp. 211–34, at p. 230.

literature investigating the nature and extent of anti-atheist discrimination in the USA. Perhaps not surprisingly, it also seems that this type of prejudice breeds yet more: for example, there is evidence that some committed atheists have a tendency towards similar stereotyping of believers, regarding them as at best innocent dupes and at worst narrow-minded and oppressive predators. One need not deny that some unbelievers really are immoral, or that some believers really are gullible bigots, to admit that neither *generalization* is remotely accurate or helpful. Clearly then, there is considerable scope here for some mutually beneficial clarification.

It would be a mistake to suppose that it is only Christians themselves who benefit from atheists better understanding them, and only atheists themselves who benefit from Christians better understanding them. Caricaturing other people's views or spreading falsehoods and damaging generalizations, reflects badly not only on those who do it but also on others in their group. Stereotypes and prejudices often have at least some basis, however weak. If some Christians become known for making false and slanderous claims about atheists, then is not difficult for most or all Christians to become tarred with same brush. In essence this is the same point as Augustine made in Chapter 3, regarding the *irrisio infidelium* or 'mockery of unbelievers'. Augustine was concerned there about Christians making 'utterly foolish and obviously untrue statements' about the natural sciences, thereby bringing not merely themselves into disrepute but Scripture and Christianity along with them. But the same surely applies to all topics that unbelievers know well 'from reason and experience', among which one may presumably include both unbelief itself, and what they and their co-non-religionists are actually like.

Once again, this works both ways. It is not, for example, only Christians who object to perceived misrepresentations of Christian doctrine and practice by certain critics. Complaining about his fellow atheists in an article titled 'Dawkins et al. bring us all into disrepute', Michael Ruse writes:

> [U]nlike the new atheists, I take scholarship seriously. I have written that *The God Delusion* made me ashamed to be an atheist and I meant it. Trying to understand how God could need no cause, Christians claim that God exists necessarily. I have taken the effort to try to understand what that means. Dawkins and company are ignorant of such claims and positively contemptuous of those who even try to understand them, let alone believe them . . . There are a lot of very bright and well informed Christian theologians. We atheists should demand no less.[14]

In common with Augustine, Ruse's point is that cheap point-scoring and wilful misunderstanding reflects badly on everyone. It also gravely undermines the trust, credibility and goodwill needed to gain the real issues one wishes to talk about a fair hearing. Ruse's primary concern, as a Darwinian philosopher and educator based in the southern USA, is with Christian acceptance of, or at least toleration of the teaching of, evolution. Augustine's was with attempting to persuade unbelievers to take the good news seriously (something we shall discuss further in the next chapter). But the same is true in either case. A serious and sympathetic attempt to

---

14 Michael Ruse, 2009, 'Dawkins et al. bring us into disrepute', *The Guardian*, 2 November. Available at: www.guardian.co.uk/commentisfree/belief/2009/nov/02/atheism-dawkins-ruse.

understand those not only *to* whom but *about* whom one is speaking is crucial to receiving a serious and sympathetic hearing. Dialogue may not be the only way to achieve this, but it is certainly one good one. Given the capacity for at least some kinds of dialogue to be public – through having a live audience, being published in magazine or book form, broadcast on radio or television or happening online via blogs or other social media – it is one that a great many people on both sides, and not just the dialoguers themselves, are able to share in and benefit from.

'O wad some Pow'r the giftie gie us . . .'

'. . . to see oursels as ithers see us! It wad frae mony a blunder free us, An' foolish notion: Wat airs in dress an' gait wad lea'e us, An' ev'n devotion!'[15] So famously wrote the Scots poet Robert Burns in his 1786 verse 'To a Louse, on Seeing One on a Lady's Bonnet at Church'. Thus far, we have focused on the potential for dialogue to inform and educate Christians' and atheists' views of each other, and the benefits that might have for both parties. Now let us consider the opportunities it holds for informing and educating Christians' and atheists' views of *themselves*. This may be dialogue's most welcome and surprising 'giftie'. A frank and honest dialogue – the kind of dialogue, perhaps, that is only possible once a significant degree of trust and candour has been slowly built up – can give us a greater appreciation of how others see us, and why.

---

15 'O would some Power the gift give us, to see ourselves as others see us! It would from many a blunder free us, and foolish notion: What airs in dress and gait would leave us, And even devotion!'

Much of this will, naturally, make for uncomfortable listening. In Chapter 3 we developed Henri de Lubac's idea that much of what Christians find dispiriting about contemporary unbelief – its extent and rapid growth, for instance, or the straw men sometimes offered up as examples of Christian belief – may well reflect ingrained failings of Christian life and thought. By extension, attentively listening to unbelievers on the topic of 'why I am not a Christian' can reveal, explicitly and implicitly, some bracing home truths. And even *if* the reasons given are based on misunderstandings, these might well still reveal deficiencies of catechesis and communication. As the Dominicans inviting Camus into their home amply understood, dialogue ought not to consist of two parties talking exclusively about themselves – at least not if either hopes to be freed from 'mony a blunder . . . An' foolish notion'.

This kind of exchange need not, however, reveal only negative or uncomfortable things. Unbelievers' perspectives on Christianity can bring to light, intentionally or not, overlooked or forgotten insights. (And the same, I suspect, is true vice versa.) Chapter 2 suggested that Christians frequently miss the startlingly radical nature of what it is that they profess. In many cases, familiarity has dulled our capacity to be shocked or excited by the claims of Christmas – a God who is a baby – or Easter – a God who gets murdered. Not so, however, those non-believers who, as in Paul's time, see in these assertions only scandalous foolishness.

In *The Crucified God*, for example, Jürgen Moltmann remarks that the true import of Good Friday

is often better recognized by non-Christians and atheists than by religious Christians, because it astonishes and offends them. They see the profane horror and godlessness of the Cross because they do not believe the religious interpretations which have given a meaning to the senselessness of this death.[16]

In that light, consider these quotations, taken from two of the New Atheists, but no doubt reflecting the views of a wider group of unbelievers. Richard Dawkins, in *The God Delusion*:

> I have described the atonement . . . as vicious, sado-masochistic and repellent. We should also dismiss it as barking mad, but for its ubiquitous familiarity which has dulled our objectivity.[17]

And Sam Harris, in a 2007 afterword to *Letter to a Christian Nation*:

> Christianity amounts to the claim that we must love and be loved by a God who approves of the scapegoating, torture, and murder of one man – his son, incidentally – in compensation for the misbehaviour and thought-crimes of all others.[18]

Now, as fair descriptions of the theology of the Cross these statements leave much to be desired. But as impressionist reflections on the *kind of thing* that the crucifixion is – a monstrous affront to, and interruption of, the

---

16 Jürgen Moltmann, [1973] 2001, *The Crucified God: The Cross of Christ as the Foundation and Criticism of Christian Theology*, trans. R. A. Wilson and John Bowden, London: SCM Press, p. 28.

17 Richard Dawkins, 2006, *The God Delusion*, London: Bantam Press, p. 253.

18 Full text available at: www.samharris.org/site/full_text/afterword-to-the-vintage-books-edition.

normal workings of the world; 'God's foolishness' as Paul puts it – they are arguably on to something vital to which Christians have inured themselves. While wonderment and incredulity are not quite the same thing, an unbeliever may yet hear strains overlooked by those with ears grown 'dull of hearing' (Matt. 13.15), and even aid them in doing the same.

Renewed appreciation for the true import of 'Christ, and him crucified' aside, seeing ourselves as others see us can have other surprising outcomes. Earlier on in this chapter, I described as a form of 'literary dialogue' the careful scholarly engagement of Christian and atheist thinkers with each other's ideas in post-war France. De Lubac's book on nineteenth-century unbelief was mentioned specifically, but there have been notable additions from the atheist side too, including Ernst Bloch's *Atheism in Christianity* (1971) and Milan Machoveč's *A Marxist Looks at Jesus* (1976). More recently, the Anglo-Swiss philosopher and journalist Alain de Botton published *Religion for Atheists: A Non-believer's Guide to the Uses of Religion* in 2012. Its central premise is 'that it must be possible to remain a committed atheist and nevertheless find religions sporadically useful, interesting, and consoling – and be curious as to the possibilities of importing certain of their ideas and practices into the secular realm'.[19] This is an unusual approach, to be sure – especially when set alongside other recent books on religion by prominent atheist intellectuals – and will repay a little attention.

While in many ways an (intentionally) odd book, *Religion for Atheists* contains numerous illuminating observations.

---

19 Alain de Botton, 2012, *Religion for Atheists: A Non-believer's Guide to the Uses of Religion*, London: Penguin, pp. 11–12.

For instance, de Botton finds much to compliment in religious approaches to education and pedagogy. Impressed by Christianity's insistence on translating difficult or abstract ideas for widespread consumption and comprehension, he comments:

> Christianity was confident that its precepts were robust enough to be understood at a variety of levels, that they could be presented in the form of crude woodcuts to the yeomen of the parish church or discussed in Latin by theologians at the University of Bologna, and that each iteration would endorse and reinforce the others . . . The greatest Christian preachers have been *vulgar* in the very best sense. While not surrendering any of their claims to complexity or insight, they have wished to help those who came to hear them.[20]

And later, he opines:

> Secular education will never succeed in reaching its potential until humanities lecturers are sent to be trained by African-American Pentecostal preachers. Only then will our timid pedagogues be able to shake off their inhibitions during lectures on Keats or Adam Smith and, unconstrained by false notions of propriety, call out to their comatose audiences, 'Do you hear me? I say do you *hear* me?' And only *then* will their now-tearful students fall to their knees, ready to let the spirit of some of the world's most important ideas enter and transform them.[21]

---

20 Botton, *Religion for Atheists*, pp. 120–1 (emphasis in original).
21 Botton, *Religion for Atheists*, pp. 131–2 (emphasis in original).

There is much else of interest and surprise in the volume – such as his extolling of Christianity's 'usefully sober vision . . . about our chances of improving on the brute facts of our corrupted natures' and his enthusiasm for the idea of a secular Stations of the Cross.[22] In many ways, and despite its own monologic presentation, *Religion for Atheists* suggests some of the more creative and lively possibilities that Christian–atheist dialogue might present. While for de Botton, 'Religions are intermittently too useful, effective and intelligent to be abandoned to the religious alone',[23] for his Christian reader, an unbeliever's eyes might perceive unnoticed 'riches hidden in secret places' (Isa. 45.3) within his or her own tradition. Neither of them, moreover, need surrender their respective unbelief or faith in order to reap these rewards. That is not, it has to be said, an inconsiderable 'giftie' at all.

Conclusion

Dialogue between Christians and atheists is, or at least has the potential to be, a rich and rewarding area. Accordingly, this chapter has attempted to do two main things. In the first place, I have tried to furnish today's burgeoning scene of Christian–atheist dialogue with a measure of background and context. Despite its reasonably deep roots, and having featured some serious 'big hitters' on both sides, it would be fair to say that this is a largely forgotten heritage. I can, for example, think of few recent instances of dialogue, or web or print comments on it, that betray any knowledge

22 Botton, *Religion for Atheists*, pp. 183, 224–6.
23 Botton, *Religion for Atheists*, p. 312.

of it. Given the accumulated wisdom of Camus, de Lubac, Machoveč, Bloch, Rahner, Moltmann and Garaudy on this score, that is surely a loss for today's dialoguers. It is primarily for their benefit, and for the encouragement of would-be dialoguers, that I have included this potted history.

Second, I have attempted to sketch out some theory to undergird Christian-atheist dialogue. In particular, I have argued that, despite the time and effort it takes to do it well, there are significant benefits to be gained all round, through the two sides both better understanding *each other* and – perhaps less obviously – better understanding *themselves*. This will only happen if dialogue partners are genuinely prepared to listen and learn from each other, and potentially to face up to troubling home truths. Thus, as one of those involved in the post-Vatican II round of dialogues put it:

> Dialogue has demanded humility, openness and trust. No real dialogue has taken place without honest self-criticism and the willingness to change. Dialogue as a *personal* encounter revealed itself to be something more than a polite and dignified exchange of opinions and informative facts.[24]

However, as was also argued a little earlier on, genuine dialogue also needs people who are not afraid to be frank and honest with each other, and are quite prepared (ideally in a respectful, constructive manner) to disagree. To put it quite simply, there are some issues that no Christian and

---

24 A. J. van der Bent, 1971, 'A Decade of Christian–Marxist Dialogue', *Ateismo e Dialogo* 6/2, pp. 22–34, at p. 22 (emphasis in original).

no atheist can ever honestly agree on – unless, that is, one party ceases to be a Christian or the other ceases to be an atheist.

What exactly those issues are may ultimately take a good deal of dialoguing to discover in full. (And this chapter has been deliberately quiet on suggested 'topics' for Christian–atheist dialogue. This is largely because there are few topics of genuine importance that are not amenable to this treatment, although some of the so-called 'big questions' – 'What is the meaning of life?', 'Why be good?', 'Where do we come from?' – might serve as good ice-breakers.) However, the idea of a person ceasing to be an atheist and, more specifically, actually becoming a Christian, while not in itself the purpose of dialogue, brings us nicely to the topic of our final chapter.

6

New evangelization?

Seventeen centuries ago, in AD 312, there lived in southern Egypt a young pagan called Pachomius. Egypt was at that time a province of the Roman Empire and, since empires need armies, it was the custom to conscript non-citizen inhabitants to serve as auxiliary soldiers. Pachomius' draft number duly came up and, along with other youths from his district, he was put in chains, loaded on to a cramped ship and transported up the Nile for training and deployment. Since these were not Roman citizens, and no one much cared if one or two died in transit, no great care was taken to keep them adequately shaded, fed or watered.

At Thebes, however, the ship stopped to load up on supplies, and Pachomius and his companions were permitted to stretch their legs on the quayside. Seeing their plight, a group of strangers came over and began to give them food and drink, showing care and concern for them as though they were long-lost relatives or friends. Astounded by this, Pachomius asked the strangers who they were and why they were so 'eager and willing to perform such humble acts of mercy' to people they had only just met. Quoting now from the ancient *Life of Pachomius*:

He was told they were Christians, who were in the habit of doing acts of kindness to everyone, but especially towards travellers. He learned also what it meant to be called a Christian. For he was told that they were godly people, followers of a genuine religion, who believed in the name of Jesus Christ the only begotten son of God, who were well disposed to all people, and hoped that God would reward them for all their good works in the life to come.[1]

Our source goes on to tell us that: 'Pachomius' heart was stirred on hearing this, and, illumined by the light of God, he felt a great attraction towards the Christian faith.' Accordingly, once his military service had ended, the young man sought catechesis and baptism, and – to cut a long story short – eventually ended up known as St Pachomius the Great, one of the founders of Christian monasticism.

What possible relevance could this narrative have for the evangelization of contemporary unbelievers? On one level, admittedly very little – after all, Pachomius wasn't an atheist, and fourth-century Egypt was a very different time and place from our own. Yet at another, deeper level, as I hope to explain throughout the course of this chapter, the evangelization of Pachomius is very germane here indeed. First, though, let us think about evangelization itself – what it is, and why it is important.

---

1 This and the other quotations in this section are taken from the late Revd Benedict Baker's wonderfully useful online translation of the *Vitae Patrum*, a seventeenth-century collection of 'lives of the Fathers' originating in the third or fourth century. The *Life of Pachomius* we have today is a sixth-century Latin translation of an earlier Greek original. The quoted sections can be found at: **www.vitae-patrum org.uk/page.11html.**

What's so good about the good news?

Jesus began his own public ministry with the manifesto: 'The time is fulfilled, and the kingdom of God has come near; repent, and believe in the good news' (Mark 1.15). In the very last words of Matthew's Gospel, he instructs his disciples: 'Go therefore and make disciples of all nations, baptizing them in the name of the Father and of the Son and of the Holy Spirit, and teaching them to obey everything that I have commanded you. And remember, I am with you always, to the end of the age' (28.19–20). From the very beginning, then, evangelization – 'good-news-ization' – has been the Christian community's very *raison d'être*. It is the Church's abiding purpose: to continue Christ's own mission to humanity, by announcing the kingdom of God, calling sinners to repentance, making disciples, baptizing, and teaching the Christian faith, safe in the knowledge that he remains 'with you always, to the end of the age'.

While that is easy enough to write, it no doubt seems far harder to put into practice. It wouldn't be so bad if we felt sure of *what*, precisely and in practical terms, we ought to set about doing. More to the point, whatever 'making disciples' might actually involve, surely it is not suited to those who feel so very un-'disciplined' themselves?

It is worth remembering that exactly the same thing was true for those Christians living in the early centuries, a time of apparently miraculous evangelistic successes. The New Testament itself paints a rather sobering picture of evangelization's difficulties and disappointments. Jesus' own Parable of the Sower (Matt. 13.1–9, 18–23) is a case in point. As Frank DeSiano perceptively comments:

Seed goes here and there, but only some of it bears fruit. The other seed seems wasted, falling on hard ground, falling among thorns, falling onto thin soil. So much wasted effort, effort that the early Christians saw in those who took on their way of life, only to abandon it because of superficiality, because of the risks and costs of Christian living, or because they just loved money more. Even the seed that does produce a yield has its hint of disappointments: only some of it yields 'a hundredfold'. The rest brings less, some considerably less.[2]

Evangelization has always been daunting, but it has also always found people willing to give it a go nonetheless. If it hadn't, not only would there be no St Pachomius to tell an anecdote about, but – even more to the present point – no one to tell it, and no one to tell it to.

This drive to go out to make known the good news requires an understanding of what evangelization is *for*. Christians do not proclaim it *only* because Jesus has told them they should. Before looking at evangelizing unbelievers specifically, it is therefore worth commenting on why Christians believe that we should evangelize anyone at all.

In the first place, the good news is, well, just that: *good news*. 'The news' is a report of recent events, and that is precisely what the first Christians ventured out from the Holy Land to spread:

- That the long-awaited Messiah had not only come, but is God himself;
- That he was born a human being and dwelt among us;

---

2 Frank P. DeSiano, 1998, *The Evangelizing Catholic: A Practical Handbook for Reaching Out*, Mahwah, NJ: Paulist Press, p. 2.

- That he came 'to bring good news to the poor . . . to proclaim release to the captives and recovery of sight to the blind, to let the oppressed go free' (Luke 4.18);
- That although betrayed, condemned and crucified, his life was given as 'a ransom for many' (Mark 10.45);
- That he has been raised as 'the firstborn of the dead' (Rev. 1.5), giving hope that we too may ultimately enter with him into 'newness of life'. (Rom. 6.4)

Those who receive these headlines as signifying 'good news' should feel an urge to share them, introducing others to the same joy and hope that they have themselves. While the news itself is only a second-hand report, it points and testifies to him who actually *embodies* 'good news of great joy for all the people' (Luke 2.10). It is impossible to become a disciple of a headline or news report, but becoming a disciple of Jesus Christ is, while challenging (cf. Matt. 16.24–26), indeed possible. The phrase 'personal relationship with Jesus Christ' is very popular among evangelical Protestants, and is rapidly gaining currency in other circles too. Certainly, it is a personal relationship – with Christ *and* others – that the 'good news' is, or ought to be, an invitation to. This whole point is made emphatically in the opening sentences of 1 John: 'we declare to you what we have seen and heard so that you also may have fellowship with us; and truly our fellowship is with the Father and with his Son Jesus Christ. We are writing these things so that our joy may be complete' (1.3).

The gospels have several different images for trying to express this kind of joy and surprise: buried treasure, a magnificent pearl, the best fishing trip ever (Matt. 13.44–48), and so on. These are the kinds of 'You'll never guess what happened to me' stories that people instinctively want to tell their friends and family not to mention strangers over the internet about. Even at a very basic and everyday level, if we come across an exciting new book or DVD box-set, we feel the urge to pass it on and share it with others. The same is, or should be, true of the good news. If we have genuinely received it as such ourselves, then evangelization – at bottom, simply telling people about this news and explaining why it is good – ought to be something that comes naturally. And if it doesn't, then this may be because we are in need of further evangelization ourselves. To give a personal example here, I can safely say that I have helped convert more people to watching *The West Wing* than I have to following Jesus Christ. Pleased as I am that several of my friends and family know the delights of Martin Sheen as President Bartlet, it seems, as I write this now, that I have gotten my evangelistic priorities terribly, terribly wrong.

The second reason, and undoubtedly the major motivator of evangelism throughout Christian history, is effectively the 'flipside' to Chapter 4. There the hope of salvation for unbelievers was discussed, and reasons were offered, rooted in both Scripture and the Christian tradition, for affirming that it is *possible* for people who are without an explicit, this-worldly faith in Christ to attain salvation. But for how many that possibility has or will become an actuality – and how many among *them* will include the contemporary atheists who are our primary concern here – is not something that we are able to judge. Some theologians, also drawing on Scripture and tradition, have argued that we can and should and must hope that all will ultimately be saved. But even so, a hope, however fervently held and prayed for, is no guarantee. Furthermore, against it one may line up a significant body of scriptural and traditional witness that not only many, *but most*, will be lost: 'Enter through the narrow gate; for the gate is wide and the road is easy that leads to destruction, and there are many who take it. For the gate is narrow and the road is hard that leads to life, and there are few who find it' (Matt. 7.13–14).

According to the Gospels, Jesus himself testifies to this link between evangelization and salvation. Hence, from the previously quoted coda to Mark's Gospel: 'Go into all the world and proclaim the good news to the whole creation. The one who believes and is baptized will be saved; but the one who does not believe will be condemned' (16.15–16). This statement alone, quite apart from any hopes to the contrary – however well-grounded – ought to give us pause. As was argued at the end of Chapter 4, while hope may indeed be justified, presumption is not. And as unfashionable and unpalatable as it might seem to say so, it is this that is the best and most urgent rationale for evangelizing today's unbelievers.

New evangelization?

On that bracing note, let us return to fourth-century Thebes. It was claimed above that evangelization was no easier in the early Church than it is today (and in many ways, of course, it was far more difficult, not to mention dangerous). But that does not entail that there are not very great differences between these two contexts. The case of Pachomius helps us to see the most important of these quite clearly. It is important to realize that, when he staggered off his ship, our twenty-something Egyptian had hitherto never met a Christian, encountered the Church or even heard the name of Jesus Christ. As an old dandruff shampoo commercial used to say, 'You never get a second chance to make a first impression'. The Theban Christians accordingly made a very good first impression indeed. For Pachomius, this was a clear case of love – indeed *caritas* – at first sight.

Throughout the past two thousand years of Christian history this, or something very like it, has been the standard mode of evangelization: proclaiming the good news to peoples who either have never heard of Christianity at all or never had any significant encounter with it. The famous, initial waves of gospel-spreading throughout Europe, Africa, the Americas, Asia and Australasia all fit within this framework. So too, necessarily, do the heroic efforts of many of the great missionaries, such as Paul, Patrick, Cyril and Methodius, Stephen of Perm, Francis Xavier, Jean de Brébeuf and Mary Bird. *This* type of evangelization remains possible, and indeed urgent, in many areas of the globe. Importantly, however, it is plainly not the situation facing would-be missionaries in the contemporary west. Here the opportunities for a 'first impression' are long, long gone. Centuries after the first waves of evangelization, the problem is no longer that people have never heard of Christianity but rather that, to their minds, they have heard quite enough.

As has been stated several times already: *generally speaking, large-scale, societal unbelief is a hallmark of Christian, or historically Christian, countries.* Consider also that significant numbers of the unbelievers in these countries will have been baptized (and perhaps confirmed), attended Christian schools or colleges and/or will have regarded themselves as being a Christian at some point in their lives (indeed, perhaps for the first couple of decades or more). And this doesn't only apply to actual atheists of one sort or another. The majority of people who would describe themselves as having 'no religion' or as being religiously 'unaffiliated' retain some form of theistic belief – that is, are not (yet?)

unbelievers – and many of these would also fit the above description. Recent statistics from the USA, for example, suggest that almost 20% of all American adults describe themselves as religious 'nones', though only about 5% would label themselves an 'atheist' or an 'agnostic'. However, only one in four American 'nones' were actually brought up as such, whereas over two-thirds of them were brought up as Christians.[3] Evidently then, these are not people for whom a Pachomius-style 'love at first sight' encounter with Christianity is possible. And that does not only apply to the former Christians among them. It is hard to imagine anyone brought up in, say, modern-day Britain, Ireland, America or Canada who has not had any significant exposure to Christianity, even if only from news reports of (mostly) scandals and crimes.

Evidently this presents challenges that are different from those faced in a traditional mission territory, and methods honed and perfected in one those may draw a blank when tried closer to home. In Catholic circles, the phrase 'new evangelization' has gradually gained currency, referring to mission aimed at 'those people who have already heard Christ proclaimed'[4] – that is, to people living in historically Christian countries. Fundamentally the same idea can be found, and often more prominently, in other denominations too. The Anabaptist theologian Stuart Murray's *Post-Christendom*,

---

3 These statistics are from the Pew Forum's 2012 *'Nones' on the Rise* study, available at: www pewforum org /unaffiliated /nones on the rise aspx. The latter statistics, not included in the report itself, were provided in a personal communication by Dr Gregory A. Smith, one of the study's lead researchers.

4 John Paul II, 1990, *Redemptoris Missio*, 30; available at: www. vatican.va/holy_father/john_paul_ii/encyclicals/documents/hf_jp-ii_enc_07121990_redemptoris-missio_en html.

for example, is a stirring reflection on evangelizing in the 'culture that emerges as the Christian faith loses coherence within a society that has been definitively shaped by the Christian story and as the institutions that have been developed to express Christian convictions decline in influence'.[5] More concretely, the Anglican and Methodist Fresh Expressions initiatives, under the slogan 'changing church for a changing world', aim explicitly at forming new communities or congregations 'especially for those who have never been involved in church (un-churched) or once were, but left for whatever reason (de-churched)'.[6] Likewise, the remarkably successful Alpha Course (begun in the Church of England in 1977 but now available across the world and in a range of denominational flavours) currently advertises itself with the words 'Don't believe in God? Given up on Church? Just Curious? Is Alpha for me? In a word, YES'.[7] Perhaps the most telling example, though, is the growing numbers, across all main denominations, of African, Asian, Caribbean or Latin American Christians coming to western Europe, Canada and the USA in order to minister and evangelize. This is a complete reversal of the historical direction of missionary work. Better than anything else, such 'reverse mission' underscores the central points of this section: that great swathes of the west are now indeed bona fide mission territories, and that this is a genuinely new and challenging turn of events.

---

5 Stuart Murray, 2004, *Post-Christendom: Church and Mission in a Strange New World*, Milton Keynes: Paternoster Press, p. 19.

6 See: www.freshexpressions.org.uk/about/whatis. A significant critique of this method can, however, be found in Andrew Davison and Alison Milbank, 2010, *For the Parish: A Critique of Fresh Expressions*, London: SCM Press.

7 See: www.alpha.org/#section -3.

What is to be done?

Evangelizing unbelievers is important and urgent. This task, in the contemporary west, presents particular difficulties of its own, quite unlike those in traditional missionary territories. All of these will require a great deal of thought, action and prayer, as well as both making and learning from a large number of mistakes. Almost certainly, moreover, we are talking here of a work of centuries rather than years.

In Chapter 3 we asked the question, 'Is it not our own fault?' and explored ways in which Christians, individually and collectively, might be to blame for the rise, persistence and plausibility of modern unbelief. The remains of this chapter will explore, in decidedly broad brushstrokes, what Christians might usefully do to remedy it. Our primary concern here is how best to introduce others to Jesus Christ. However, as the parable's eponymous Sower learned the hard way, the nature of the soil is crucial to the success or failure of the whole enterprise. The point here is that ideas or arguments are not heard in a vacuum; rather, they are received – or not – against a complex background of social, cultural, historical and personal factors. To give a fairly crude example: no matter how tightly argued and well-evidenced a given piece of apologetic preaching may be, it will struggle to find a serious hearing in a world in which everyone 'just knows' that Christianity is at best backward and outdated, and at worst, evil and corrupt. Simply giving 'an accounting for the hope that is in you' (1 Peter 3.15), in the narrow sense, is unlikely to suffice. We need, therefore, to turn our attention to the context in which we give our accountings. Before we preach the good news, we must do our best to 'prepare the way' so that it (or rather he) is received *as* good news. And on that note, let us return to Pachomius.

Practising what we preach

Pachomius' first contact with Christianity was not with an argument, idea or piece of apologetic 'accounting'. Rather, it was a direct face-to-face encounter with Christian *caritas* or love. In effect, he met with the fourth-century Theban equivalent of the parish 'soup run' or Society of St Vincent de Paul: ordinary believers doing what little they are able for 'the least of these who are members of my family' (Matt. 25.40).

Throughout the first centuries of the Church, we find evidence of people being converted by the example of Christians *living out* the implications of their Faith. Already in Acts we find a clear connection between a) the earliest Christians' practice of giving 'to all, as any had need', b) their receiving 'the goodwill of all the people', and c) the fact that 'day by day the Lord added to their number those who were being saved' (2.44–47). Note particularly here the explicit link between Christian living, the influence this had on the wider socio-cultural context ('all the people'), and ultimate evangelistic success. According to Tertullian, by the early third century Christians had become widely known for 'our care for the derelict and our active love': '"See", [the pagans] say, "how they love one another . . . how ready they are even to die for one another"' (*Apology*, 39).[8] And though one might reasonably suspect Christian writers of bias here, we have supporting testimonies from non-Christians too. For instance, the second-century satirist Lucian of Samosata's mockery of Christians' generosity

---

8 Quoted from Alexander Roberts and James Donaldson (eds), 1996, *The Ante-Nicene Fathers, Volume 3: Latin Christianity: Its Founder, Tertullian; I. Apologetic; II. Anti-Marcion; III. Ethical*, Edinburgh: T & T Clark, p. 46.

and (to his mind) gullibility evidently draws on widespread beliefs concerning their trust and largesse:

> The poor fools have persuaded themselves above all that they are immortal and will live forever, from which it follows that they despise death and many of them willingly undergo imprisonment. Moreover, their first lawgiver taught them that they are all brothers of one another . . . So, they despise all things equally and regard them as common property . . . Accordingly, if any quack of trickster, who can press his advantage, comes among them, he can acquire great wealth in a very short time by imposing on simple-minded people. (*Peregrinus*, 13)[9]

Most revealing of all, however, is the fourth-century Emperor Julian, who renounced his Christian upbringing in order to restore the old Roman gods. In a 362 letter to the pagan high priest of Galatia, he complains of the Christians' successes with evangelization:

> Why do we not observe that it is their benevolence to strangers, their care for the graves of the dead, and the pretended holiness of their lives that have done most to increase atheism [i.e. Christianity]? . . . For it is disgraceful that . . . the impious Galileans support not only their own poor, but ours as well.[10]

---

9 Quoted from C. D. N. Costa (trans.), 2009, *Lucian: Selected Dialogues*, Oxford: Oxford University Press, p. 77.

10 Quoted from Ralph Martin Novak, 2001, *Christianity and the Roman Empire: Background Texts*, Harrisburg, PA: Trinity Press, p. 183.

Significantly for our purposes here, the witness of Christian living did not only attract those encountering Christianity for the first time, like Pachomius, it also changed the minds of those who had already heard a lot of bad things about Christians. As we saw in Chapter 1, this was true of Justin Martyr. For him, it was not Christian charity directly but rather the brave conduct of the martyrs in the Roman arenas (an impression to which Lucian, quoted above, also bears witness) that caused him to think again. In the fullness of time, Justin himself, scourged then beheaded by the Romans in about the year 165, gave up his own life as a witness for many.

The basic point being made here is nothing remotely new in the history of missiology. The Church has long recognized the necessity of living out what we claim to profess, and the potency this can have for evangelization. St Ignatius of Antioch, writing at the very beginning of the second century, advised 'No doubt it is a fine thing to instruct others, but only if the speaker practises what he preaches' (*Ephesians*, 15).[11] According to St Leo the Great in the fifth century, 'examples are stronger than words, and there is more teaching in practice than in precept' (*Sermon* 85).[12] Likewise, the Rule of St Francis advises 'Let all the brothers . . . preach by their deeds.'[13] This is probably the source of the famous injunction, often attributed to Francis but most likely of recent coinage, to 'preach the gospel at all times; use words

---

11 Quoted from Maxwell Staniforth (trans.), 1968, *Early Christian Writings*, Harmondsworth: Penguin, p. 80.

12 Quoted from Philip Schaff and Henry Wace (eds), 1999, *Nicene and Post-Nicene Fathers, Volume 12: Leo the Great, Gregory the Great*, Peabody, MA: Hendrickson, p. 197.

13 Quoted from Regis J. Armstrong et al. (eds and trans.), 1999, *St Francis: The Saint, Volume I*, New York: New City Press, p. 75.

if necessary'. The same idea is behind the oft-quoted words of Pope Paul VI: 'Modern man listens more willingly to witnesses than to teachers, and if he does listen to teachers, it is because they are witnesses.'[14]

The fact that this idea is an old one does not preclude it from also being, or being made, new. There are strong grounds for thinking that these kinds of concerns are even more important now than in ages past. As explored in Chapter 3, perhaps the most prominent and powerful criticisms by contemporary unbelievers are not intellectual but moral ones. This can clearly be seen, for example, in the writings of the New Atheists. While *The God Delusion* makes comparatively short work of the intellectual arguments for or against God's existence (largely because Dawkins thinks there is very little of real substance there anyway), explicitly ethical concerns are a key driver of the book's overall passion and urgency. Christianity – along with every other religion – is depicted not as false but benign, but rather as something actively harmful and morally corrupting, in both theory and practice. As we know all too well, subscribers to this kind of opinion, who are by no means confined to the New Atheists alone, have no shortage of concrete examples they can offer up in support.

Consider again, therefore, our idea of there being a 'socio-cultural background' against which the good news is heard (or not). Without putting too fine a point on it, it would be fair to say that, *for very understandable reasons*, our Christian communities are not held in universally high moral regard at the present time. This is true enough among

---

14 Paul VI, 1975, *Evangelii Nuntiandi*, 41; available at: www.vatican.va/holy_father/paul_vi/apost_exhortations/documents/hf_p-vi_exh_19751208_evangelii-nuntiandi_en html.

Christians themselves, let alone actual unbelievers. Hence it would be not just piously, but absurdly, wishful thinking to hope for a time when, as testified to by Lucian in the second century, the popular stereotype of Christians is that they are far *too* moral, so extravagantly generous and unworldly as to be easy prey for tricksters. Likewise, the notion that Christians as a whole might one day soon not only gain, but actually deserve, 'the goodwill of all the people' à la Acts 2 is pure fantasy. 'You never get a second chance to make a first impression', after all.

Thankfully, even against such a dark and unpromising backdrop, it is possible for individuals, or acts, to stand out. Heroic figures are, obviously, important here. The witness of a Mother Teresa, Dorothy Day, Desmond Tutu, Susan Clarkson, Shay Cullen or Albert Schweitzer prevents Christianity being entirely written off as morally moribund and socially useless. Such figures signal to the world, as well as to us, that there might be some wheat among the chaff after all. And while the 'works of mercy' – feeding the hungry, giving drink to the thirsty, clothing the naked, welcoming the stranger and visiting the sick and imprisoned (cf. Matt. 25.35–36) – are not undertaken for the purposes of evangelization, we need not be blind to their potency in 'preparing the way'. As noted in Chapter 3 regarding Christian hypocrisy, there is a growing body of social-scientific research exploring the evolutionary reasons why living out the implications of a particular belief renders that belief more persuasive to others.

It would be wrong, however, to suppose that this kind of concrete witness is rightly or exclusively the preserve of 'the saints' – and especially not if we (wrongly) understand by that phrase a discrete class of 'super-Christians', set apart from the rest of us. Remember who the heroes of our fourth-century anecdote are: *not* the future St Pachomius the Great but rather the nameless and nondescript believers who met him at the quayside (cf. 1 Cor. 1.26–29). They can have had no premonition of the long-term repercussions of their actions in either the life of Pachomius or the history of the Church. All they did was give a scared young man their time, attention and a little something to eat and drink. Possibly they did this every day; maybe this was the only time. But importantly, they did nothing beyond what a large number of equally 'ordinary' Christians do on a more or less regular basis. Christians ought to do these things anyway. From the (secondary) perspective of evangelization, however, these are instances of putting one's faith into practice – doing good deeds *because* one is a Christian;[15] practising what one preaches; being a witness – and this constitutes an important form of 'prepar[ing] the way of the LORD' (Isa. 40.3). This is a small but indispensable contribution to the context in which the good news is proclaimed and received.

Preaching what we practise

That said, it is necessary to recognize that, crucial though the Theban Christians' *witness* was, it was not that witness itself that set Pachomius on the path to baptism. His brief encounter with Christian love-in-action both prompted him to ask the question, 'Who are you and why are you doing this?' and gave him cause to listen attentively to the answer he received. But according to our source it was the answer *itself* that actually 'stirred' Pachomius' heart and, 'illumined by

---

15 This is not, of course, to imply that non-Christians do not do good deeds, albeit for other reasons.

the light of God', made him feel 'a great attraction towards the Christian faith'. This short answer, quoted in full earlier in this chapter, is a minor masterpiece of evangelization: simple and concise, hope-filled yet humble, unwilling to water down difficult ideas (e.g. 'only begotten son of God'), but without resorting to jargon-filled obscurity.

The point is a very simple one. In the words of St Paul: 'But how are they to call on one in whom they have not believed? And how are they to believe in one of whom they have never heard? And how are they to hear without someone to proclaim him?' (Rom. 10.14). While Paul is referring here to his fellow Jews, the sentiment applies to all non-Christians, not excepting our contemporary atheist friends and relatives. It has been remarked several times in this book that since even basic Christian doctrines are often not well understood or appreciated by Christians themselves, it is not surprising that unbelievers' representations of them are sometimes similarly flawed. Correcting these kinds of misapprehensions, showing why they are wrong and outlining what Christians really believe, are the primary tasks of evangelization. Yet in order to do this we must first of all ensure that we, along with other believers, have a solid grounding in Christian doctrine ourselves. Catechesis cannot, therefore, really be understood as something that is separate from evangelization. Furthermore, since a significant number of non-believers have themselves been brought up as Christians, better education in the faith to begin with ought to lessen our task some years down the line.

There is, however, no use in putting off the inevitable: if we are serious about evangelizing unbelievers, then we need to be prepared actually to talk to them about our faith directly. This is something that many Christians feel shy or uncomfortable about, even when among other Christians. There can be many reasons for this. Many people probably don't feel confident enough about what it is they (are supposed to) believe and why it is they (are supposed to) believe it. Or maybe, when speaking to non-Christians, they don't want to come across as proselytizing or being 'preachy'. It might be that they fear that others will think them judgemental, bigoted or irrational for adhering either to Christianity itself or to some particular doctrine. Or possibly their faith feels too 'personal' to be the subject of general chitchat. Increasingly, perhaps, people think that they will be mocked or sneered at for saying what they really believe. All of these reasons are natural and understandable. Unfortunately, Christians are encouraged to 'Always be ready to make your defence to anyone who demands from you an account of the hope that is in you; yet do it with gentleness and reverence' (1 Peter 3.15–16). That is, I fully admit, far easier said than done. Even so, it is something that, in mostly ordinary and everyday ways, is within reach of all of us.

First of all, note again how the Theban Christians were responding to Pachomius' own question. They were therefore innocent of one of today's seemingly most heinous sins: 'pushing their views on others' or 'ramming it down their throats'. As mentioned above, this is something that Christians are often very coy about, and perhaps rightly so. Nobody much likes being preached at, and overly enthusiastic evangelizers run the risk of alienating far more people than they attract. It is also true, however, that questions about what one believes and why are often motivated by a genuine and interested curiosity. Faced with such enquiries, many believers try to deflect them with some bland, self-effacing or tongue-in-cheek reply. For some of the reasons outlined above, this is an understandable habit, but it is also an unhelpful one, not least to one's questioner. Suppose, for example, that Pachomius' question had been met with a mumbled 'Oh well, I don't really know . . . I suppose it's just what anyone would do, isn't it? Gets us out the house, keeps us out of trouble, I guess! I mean, we *are* from a "church", but that's not something we really like to push on people . . .' As an 'account of the hope that is in you', while one cannot fault its 'gentleness', this kind of answer exhibits little real 'reverence' for the good faith and sincerity of the person asking.

Second, it happens frequently enough that one reads or hears things ascribed to Christians or Christianity itself that are either false, partial or miss the point in some major way. While this is sometimes done in a polemical or aggressive way, often it is simply done in passing, as a bland state- ment of presumed fact. In both cases, Christians need to feel confident enough in their own understanding of the topic, and bold enough – with due 'gentleness and reverence' – to offer a correction. 'Instructing the ignorant' has, after all, long been recognized as one of the spiritual works of mercy (along with, be it noted, 'bearing wrongs patiently' and 'for- giving offences willingly'). This could apply to a dauntingly wide range of topics, though perhaps at the present time teachings on marriage, the family, sexuality, abortion, con- traception and questions of religious freedom are likely to be prominent. These are complex issues, and there is no one, universally agreed 'Christian position' on any of them: dif- ferent Christians, from different denominations, hold differ- ent views on all of them.[16] Each one of these Christian views, however, is no doubt open to misunderstanding and misrep- resentation, requiring a patient and careful explanation as to

---

16 That said, this does not mean that there is no single, *correct* view on any of them either. One can recognize an honest diversity of opin- ion without committing oneself to relativism. However, this is a question regarding ecumenical dialogue rather than the evangelization of atheists.

how and why this is the case. In order to be successful, such an explanation need not actually *persuade* one's conversation partners of the truth of the given Christian position. In many cases it will be enough to show that Christians do not, as a matter of fact, hold the perhaps irrational and ridiculous stance that is being ascribed to them. This point again relates to Augustine's and Thomas' cautioning concerning the 'mockery of unbelievers'. One's unbelieving interlocutors will probably still disagree with the Christian position. Hopefully, though, they will have gained a new appreciation of the reason and evidence undergirding it.

Naturally, this does not only apply to the 'hot button' moral, social and political issues of the day. Many of Christianity's core tenets – those held in common by most or all mainstream denominations – are likewise often the victims of misunderstanding and misrepresentation, whether wilfully or by accident. Correcting these kinds of errors is even more crucial to the overall task of evangelization. Evidently, it is one thing for an atheist to realize that a particular stance on marriage or contraception actually makes sense, at least as part of an overarching Christian vision. But it is quite another for him or her to realize that the overarching vision *itself* makes sense, and that for all its apparent 'foolishness', it too is undergirded by reason and evidence.

To take just one example here, one commonly hears the core notion of 'faith' itself being cited by non-believers as proof of Christian antipathy towards reason and evidence. On this widespread (mis)understanding, faith is understood to mean 'believing in things even when common sense tells you not to' (*The Miracle on 34th Street*, 1955 version), or 'believing in the absence of evidence, even in the teeth of evidence.'[17] This is absurd. If faith really did mean what the above definitions claim, then saying to someone 'I have faith in you' should be taken as an insult, since it would be an admission that you have no reason whatsoever for believing that they'll do whatever it is they've said they will. Instead, 'faith' is derived from the Latin word *fides*, the root meaning of which is 'trust'. (This is where words such as con*fide* and con*fide*nce, both of which have to do with being 'with-trust' regarding someone or something, come from. The same applies to trusting, loyal, faithful dogs named 'Fido'.)

Trust can be well-placed or misplaced. Suppose a student assures me she will definitely submit her essay before tomorrow's deadline. If I know she hasn't even started it yet, and every essay she has ever submitted has been months late, then I would probably be wrong to trust, or have faith in, her word. But if she has only the proofreading still to do, and has always previously been punctiliously punctual, I have every reason to have faith in her. Christian faith, likewise, is not – or at least is not intended to be – something opposed to evidence and reason but rather, like all forms of trusting ought to be, is built upon them. And since our 'hope' is one that is founded on faith, establishing the nature of this foundation is an indispensable part of our 'accounting'. Only once this has been clarified is it possible to open up a conversation – even perhaps some months, or years, down the line – about the kinds of reasons and evidences that undergird Christians' trust.

---

17 Richard Dawkins, [1976] 1989, *The Selfish Gene*, 2nd edn, Oxford: Oxford University Press, p. 198.

Conclusion

This chapter has outlined the case for evangelization – what it is for and why it is so important – and also offered some preliminary observations on how Christians might begin to set about actually doing this. 'Preliminary' and 'begin' are the operative words here: evangelization has never been an easy task, and the new evangelization comes with challenges of its own. But since the Church exists in order to evangelize, this is no excuse for not even trying.

Using the example of St Pachomius (or rather, the example of those nameless, ordinary believers who made 'St' Pachomius possible), particular emphasis was given to the need to both 'practise what we preach' *and* 'preach what we practise' – to be witnesses *and* teachers – as a solid principle for all evangelization, and as being particularly relevant in the face of contemporary unbelief. Along the way, a number of practical, concrete pointers were advanced as worthwhile and (relatively?) stress-free first attempts, within reasonable reach of all Christian believers. Special attention has been given in these to the laying of a groundwork: 'preparing the way of the Lord' by confounding expectations of Christian hypocrisy with our own actions (however feeble and faltering these may seem), and presenting 'gentle and reverent' corrections to misunderstandings concerning Christian beliefs. In the latter case, I am aware of the overlap between what is described here as 'evangelization' and much of what was described in the previous chapter as 'dialogue'. This should not surprise us. For while the purpose of dialogue is not, in itself, an evangelistic one, through correcting misconceptions and defusing the 'mockery of unbelievers', it too contributes to making the good news of Jesus Christ – 'the hope that is in you' – better known and appreciated.

Implicit in this chapter is the view that evangelization comes in many, and often subtle, forms. Standing on a soapbox in the town square announcing the coming of the Lord, or going door-to-door asking people if they have a personal relationship with Jesus, are certainly two ways – and God bless those with the courage to attempt them. But they are not the only ones. There is much that one can do to help spread the good news to unbelievers that we have barely touched upon, if at all. Little has been said, for example, about the challenges and opportunities presented by the internet (although much that has been said applies here too, especially the bit about 'gentleness and reverence'), the merits of inviting unbelieving friends along to church-related events to 'come and see' or even about apologetics in any sustained or systematic manner. While this has partly been for reasons of space and concision, it is mainly been due to a desire to focus on fundamentals. Detailed knowledge of the argument from cosmic fine-tuning, of the varying explanations of the empty tomb or of the possibilities of viral marketing using social media are undoubtedly fine and effective tools for the new evangelization. But they will all be of severely stunted use if Christians don't regard evangelization as something important or 'for them', if they neglect the works of mercy or if, for fear of seeming 'preachy', they shrink from politely correcting an unbelieving friend or relative's supposition that faith – the cornerstone of the good news, upon which everything else is built – 'means believing in things even when common sense tells you not to'.

Afterword

This book began with Paul's reminder to the Gentile converts of Ephesus of when they were 'strangers to the covenants of promise, having no hope and *atheoi* in the world'
(Eph. 2.12). As we have seen, whatever Paul intended by
the term – and he is the only one of the New Testament
authors to use it – he was certainly not referring to *atheists* in anything like the contemporary, English meaning of
the term. The same is true of the early Church fathers. For
them, *atheos* could refer either to pagan polytheists (on the
lips of St Polycarp) or to Christians themselves, whether as
a jeering insult from its detractors (like the Emperor Julian)
or as a proud self-designation (as with St Justin's 'we confess
that we are *atheoi*'). For these foundational Christian thinkers, however, atheism in our modern sense – an absence of
belief in the existence of a God or gods – was an almost
unheard-of notion, and would largely remain as such until
the Enlightenment.

Does this mean that both Scripture and the great bulk of
the Christian tradition have nothing significant to say to
us regarding contemporary unbelief? *Not at all.* Nuclear
weapons, renewable energy, stem-cell research, development economics, space exploration and Darwinian evolution were equally unknown to the evangelists, Paul,

Tertullian, Augustine and Aquinas. While others may disagree, Christians are convinced that these authors' writings hold a great deal of relevance to the many, diverse and highly complex questions thrown up by all these topics and many more. The same is certainly true of what, as early as fifty years ago, Vatican II recognized to be 'among the most serious problems of this age, and . . . deserving of closer examination' (*Gaudium et Spes*, 19).

'Deserving of closer examination' is an important phrase. It is clearly inadequate for Christians to presume that they have something worthwhile to say about contemporary atheism and atheists, without having first made a genuine effort to understand them. Naturally, one would be ill-advised to opine theologically on the ethical implications of stem-cell research or the benefits of microfinance schemes in the developing world, without first doing a bit of reading up on them (at the very least). No amount of quoting Scripture or the Church fathers will help Christians make sense of these complex issues if – as Augustine cautions us – 'they don't understand either what they are saying or the things about which they are making assertions' (*Literal Interpretation*, I, xix, 39; quoting 1 Tim. 1.7). Likewise, if Christians want to think about contemporary unbelievers in a way befitting disciples of the Most True God – if they really want to speak and write about modern atheists in a manner that is *radical enough* to be fully orthodox – then they need to take the time and trouble both to learn about and dialogue with those of whom they speak. This book is intended as an invitation to do just that.

Finally, I have spoken in these pages of there being a fault line between faith and unbelief in our contemporary, western societies. Fault lines can be unnerving and tumultuous places, prone to tremors, earthquakes and volcanic eruptions. But they can also be very creative, as the world's great mountain ranges, from the Appalachians to the Himalayas, dramatically testify. In essence, a fault line – whether literal or metaphorical – is a place of contact, where two major bodies 'rub along together' in a (normally) peaceable way. It is worth remembering that, from the Christian perspective at least, occasional friction is vastly preferable to the alternative: a gradual, relentless and ultimately permanent *drifting away*.

Further reading

This book has touched upon a wide range of topics, some in depth and many more in passing. Most of these have a large and growing corpus of literature attached to them. The suggestions below are offered as being of possible interest to those wanting to follow up on some of the book's more prominent themes. Many of them have informed and influenced the ideas in these pages.

Introductions to the theology of atheism
Michael Paul Gallagher, 1995, *What Are They Saying About Unbelief?*, Mahwah, NJ: Paulist Press.

Contemporary atheism: general
Julian Baggini, 2003, *Atheism: A Very Short Introduction*, Oxford: Oxford University Press.

Michael Martin (ed.), 2007, *The Cambridge Companion to Atheism*, Cambridge: Cambridge University Press.

Kerry Walters, 2010, *Atheism: A Guide for the Perplexed*, New York: Continuum.

New Atheism
Richard Dawkins, 2006, *The God Delusion*, London: Bantam Press.

Sam Harris, 2004, *The End of Faith: Religion, Terror, and the Future of Reason*, New York: Norton.

Christopher Hitchens, 2007, *God is Not Great: How Religion Poisons Everything*, New York: Twelve.

Responses to the New Atheism

Tina Beattie, 2007, *The New Atheists: The Twilight of Reason and the War on Religion*, London: Darton, Longman & Todd.

Terry Eagleton, 2009, *Reason, Faith and Revolution: Reflections on the God Debate*, New Haven, CT: Yale University Press.

David Bentley Hart, 2010, *Atheist Delusions: The Christian Revolution and its Fashionable Enemies*, New Haven, CT: Yale University Press.

Ian Markham, 2010, *Against Atheism: Why Dawkins, Hitchens, and Harris Are Fundamentally Wrong*, Chichester: Wiley-Blackwell.

Keith Ward, 2008, *Why There Almost Certainly Is a God: Doubting Dawkins*, Oxford: Lion Hudson.

Early Church

Mark J. Edwards, 2013, 'The First Millennium', in Stephen Bullivant and Michael Ruse (eds), *The Oxford Handbook of Atheism*, Oxford: Oxford University Press.

Morwenna Ludlow, 2009, *The Early Church*, London: I. B. Tauris.

Maxwell Staniforth (ed. and trans.), 1968, *Early Christian Writings*, Harmondsworth: Penguin.

Robert Louis Wilken, 2003, *The Christians as the Romans Saw Them*, 2nd edn, New Haven, CT: Yale University Press.

Fyodor Dostoevsky

Fyodor Dostoevsky, [1872] 2000, *Demons*, trans. Richard Pevear and Larissa Volokhonsky, New York: Everyman.

Fyodor Dostoevsky, [1880] 2004, *The Brothers Karamazov*, trans. Richard Pevear and Larissa Volokhonsky, London: Vintage.

Malcolm Jones, 2005, *Dostoevsky and the Dynamics of Religious Experience*, London: Anthem Press.

Rowan Williams, 2010, *Dostoevsky: Language, Faith and Fiction*, London: Continuum.

'Darkness' and Christian spirituality

Guy Gaucher, 1990, *The Passion of St Thérèse of Lisieux*, trans. Anne-Marie Brennan, New York: Crossroad.

Addison Hodges Hart, 2009, *Knowing Darkness: On Skepticism, Melancholy, Friendship, and God*, Grand Rapids, MI: Eerdmans.

Brian Kolodiejchuk (ed.), 2008, *Mother Teresa: Come Be My Light: The Revealing Private Writings of the Nobel Peace Prize Winner*, London: Rider.

Kaye P. McKee, 2006, *When God Walks Away: A Companion for the Journey through the Dark Night of the Soul*, New York: Crossroad.

Peter Tyler, 2010, *St John of the Cross*, London: Continuum.

The problem of evil

Marilyn McCord Adams, 2006, *Horrendous Evils and the Goodness of God*, Ithaca, NY: Cornell University Press.

Michael L. Peterson, 2013, 'The Problem of Evil', in Stephen Bullivant and Michael Ruse (eds), *The Oxford Handbook of Atheism*, Oxford: Oxford University Press.

Stewart R. Sutherland, 1977, *Atheism and the Rejection of God: The Brothers Karamazov and Contemporary Philosophy*, Oxford: Blackwell.

Science and religion

Paul Davies, 2007, *The Goldilocks Enigma: Why is the Universe Just Right for Life?*, London: Penguin.

James Hannam, 2010, *God's Philosophers: How the Medieval World Laid the Foundations of Modern Science*, London: Icon.

John F. Haught, 2000, *God After Darwin: A Theology of Evolution*, Boulder, CO: Westview Press.

Michael Ruse, 2004, *Can a Darwinian be a Christian? The Relationship Between Science and Religion*, 2nd edn, Cambridge: Cambridge University Press.

Enlightenment origins of atheism

Michael J. Buckley, 1987, *At the Origins of Modern Atheism*, New Haven, CT: Yale University Press.

Michael J. Buckley, 2004, *Denying and Disclosing God: The Ambiguous Progress of Modern Atheism*, New Haven, CT: Yale University Press.

Gavin Hyman, 2010, *A Short History of Atheism*, London: I. B. Tauris.

Alan Charles Kors, 2013, 'The Age of Enlightenment', in Stephen Bullivant and Michael Ruse (eds), *The Oxford Handbook of Atheism*, Oxford: Oxford University Press.

Secularization

Callum G. Brown and Michael Snape (eds), 2010, *Secularisation in the Christian World*, Aldershot: Ashgate.

Steve Bruce, 2011, *Secularization: In Defence of an Unfashionable Theory*, Oxford: Oxford University Press.

Grace Davie, 2002, *Europe: The Exceptional Case: Parameters of Faith in the Modern World*, London: Darton, Longman & Todd.

Rob Warner, 2010, *Secularization and its Discontents*, London: Continuum.

Vatican II on atheism

Stephen Bullivant, 2011, 'Atheism, Apologetics and Ecclesiology: *Gaudium et Spes* and Contemporary Unbelief', in Andrew Davison (ed.), *Imaginative Apologetics: Theology, Philosophy and the Catholic Tradition*, Norwich: SCM Press.

Peter Hebblethwaite, 1967, *The Council Fathers and Atheism: The Interventions at the Fourth Session of Vatican Council II*, New York: Paulist Press.

Religion (and non-religion) in the USA

Ryan Cragun et al., 2012, 'On the Receiving End: Discrimination towards the Nonreligious', *Journal of Contemporary Religion* 27/1, pp. 105–27.

Frank Newport, 2012, *God is Alive and Well: The Future of Religion in America*, New York: Gallup Press.

David Niose, 2012, *Nonbeliever Nation: The Rise of Secular Americans*, New York: Palgrave Macmillan.

Robert D. Putnam and David E. Campbell, 2012, *American Grace: How Religion Divides and Unites Us*, New York: Simon & Schuster.

Salvation of non-Christians

Stephen Bullivant, 2012, *The Salvation of Atheists and Catholic Dogmatic Theology*, Oxford: Oxford University Press.

Jean Daniélou, 1957, *Holy Pagans in the Old Testament*, trans. Felix Faber, London: Longmans, Green & Co.

Gavin D'Costa, Paul Knitter and Daniel Strange, 2011, *Only One Way? Three Christian Responses to the Uniqueness of Christ in a Religiously Pluralist World*, London: SCM Press.

Gerald O'Collins, 2008, *Salvation for All: God's Other Peoples*, Oxford: Oxford University Press.

Karl Rahner, [1964] 1969, 'Anonymous Christians', *Theological Investigations, Volume VI*, trans. Karl-H. and Boniface Kruger, London: Darton, Longman & Todd.

Francis A. Sullivan, 1992, *Salvation Outside the Church? Tracing the History of the Catholic Response*, London: Geoffrey Chapman.

Universal salvation (recent debates)

Hans Urs von Balthasar, 1988, *Dare We Hope That "All Men Be Saved"?*, trans. David Kipp and Lothar Krauth, San Francisco, CA: Ignatius Press.

Rob Bell, 2011, *Love Wins: At the Heart of Life's Big Questions*, New York: Collins.

Howard Dorgan, 1997, *In the Hands of a Happy God: The 'No-Hellers' of Central Appalachia*, Knoxville, TN: University of Tennessee Press.

Ralph Martin, 2012, *Will Many Be Saved? What Vatican II Actually Teaches and its Implications for the New Evangelization*, Grand Rapids, MI: Eerdmans.

John R. Sachs, 1993, 'Apocatastasis in Patristic Theology', *Theological Studies* 54, pp. 617–40.

Christian-atheist dialogue (history)

Oscar L. Arnal, 1984, *Priests in Working-Class Blue: The History of the Worker-Priests (1943–1954)*, Mahwah, NJ: Paulist Press.

Ernst Bloch, 1972, *Atheism in Christianity*, trans. J. T. Swann, New York: Herder & Herder.

Stephen Bullivant, 2009, 'From "*Main Tendue*" to Vatican II: the Catholic Engagement with Atheism, 1936–65', *New Blackfriars* 90/1026, pp. 178–87.

Giovanni Guareschi, [1948] 2002, *The Little World of Don Camillo*, trans. Una Vincenzo Troubridge, Mattituck, NY: Amereon.

Peter Hebblethwaite, 1977, *The Christian–Marxist Dialogue: Beginnings, Present Status and Beyond*, London: Darton, Longman & Todd.

Henri de Lubac, [1944] 1995, *The Drama of Atheist Humanism*, trans. Edith M. Riley, Anne Englund Nash and Mark Sebanc, San Francisco, CA: Ignatius Press.

Milan Machoveč, 1976, *A Marxist Looks at Jesus*, London: Darton, Longman & Todd.

Christian-atheist dialogue (recent)

Umberto Eco and Carlo Maria Martini, 2000, *Belief or Non-Belief? A Confrontation*, trans. Minna Procter, London: Continuum.

Luis Palau and Zhao Qizheng, 2008, *A Friendly Dialogue Between a Christian and an Atheist*, Grand Rapids, MI: Zondervan.

Joseph Ratzinger and Jürgen Habermas, 2007, *The Dialectics of Secularization: On Reason and Religion*, trans. Brian McNeill, San Francisco, CA: Ignatius Press.

James W. Sire and Chris Peraino, 2009, *Deepest Differences: A Christian–Atheist Dialogue*, Westmont, IL: InterVarsity Press.

Slavoj Žižek and John Milbank, 2009, *The Monstrosity of Christ: Paradox or Dialectic?*, ed. Creston Davis, Boston, MA: MIT Press.

New evangelization

Austen Ivereigh, 2012, *How to Defend the Faith without Raising Your Voice: Civil Responses to Catholic Hot Button Issues*, Huntington, IN: Our Sunday Visitor.

Andrew Davison (ed.), 2011, *Imaginative Apologetics: Theology, Philosophy and the Catholic Tradition*, Norwich: SCM Press.

Michael Green, 2003, *Evangelism in the Early Church*, rev. edn, Eastbourne: Kingsway Publications.

George Weigel, 2013, *Evangelical Catholicism: Deep Reform in the 21st-Century Church*, New York: Basic Books.

Index